# WORLD WAR II
# IN THE
# ATLANTIC

# WORLD WAR II
# IN THE
# ATLANTIC

## CHARLES MESSENGER

Published by Warfare
An imprint of Books & Toys Ltd.
The Grange
Grange Yard
London SE1 3AG

Produced by
Bison Books Ltd
Kimbolton House
117A Fulham Road
London SW3 6RL

ISBN 0-8317-6025-7

Printed in Hong Kong

10 9 8 7 6 5 4 3 2 1

PAGE 1: Günther Prien, who
sank the British battleship
*Royal Oak*, leaves the
French Atlantic port of
Lorient in *U-47* bound for
the North Atlantic,
November 1940.

PAGES 2-3: An Atlantic
convoy prepares to sail.

THESE PAGES: The destroyer
HMS *Walker* acting as a
convoy escort.

# CONTENTS

# INTRODUCTION

As an island, Britain has always been heavily reliant on the sea. Indeed, her lifeblood has traditionally flowed through the sea routes which connect her to the rest of the world. This has been repeatedly recognized by her enemies in war. Both during the Seven Years and Napoleonic Wars France made efforts to throttle Britain's maritime trade routes by attacking her merchant vessels. The most effective defense against this was found to be convoying, giving merchant ships protection by sailing them in groups under naval escort.

Up until the late nineteenth century the threat to shipping had been solely a surface one, but the development of aircraft and, more especially, submarines in the years leading up to World War I suddenly made naval warfare a far more complex business. At the outbreak of war, however, neither the Royal nor German Navies saw either as much of a threat. The first clash between a surface vessel and a submarine occurred five days after Britain had declared war, when the light cruiser *Birmingham* caught the German U-boat (*Untersee Boote*) *U-15* on the surface and rammed her. Not until a few weeks later did the U-boat begin to show its true potential. On 6 September the flotilla leader *Pathfinder* was sunk by *U-21*, but worse was to follow. On the 22nd, in the space of 75 minutes, *U-9* sank the elderly cruisers *Hogue*, *Crecy* and *Aboukir* off the Dutch coast with heavy loss of life. Then, on 20 October 1914, came the first sinking of a merchant vessel, when *U-17* stopped the British steamer *Glitra* off

the coast of Norway, ordered her crew into their lifeboats and opened her seacocks. This was in accordance with international law, which stressed that the crew of a merchant vessel must be put in a place of safety before she was sunk by a warship.

By the end of the year U-boats had sunk some 10 merchant vessels, but their prime target remained enemy warships. It was only after the German surface raiders in the South Atlantic and Pacific had been caught and dealt with during the closing months of 1914 that the German Navy began to urge a policy of unrestricted submarine warfare against Allied merchant shipping. On 4 February 1915 the German government succumbed to this pressure and declared a war zone around the British Isles. Any merchant vessel entering it, flying whatever flag, risked being sunk without warning. In the next two-and-a-half months 39 merchant vessels were sunk, culminating on 7 May, when *U-20* sank the US liner *Lusitania*. Among the 1198 victims were 128 Americans, but official US protests were brushed aside by the Germans, who stated that ample warning had been given. The sinkings continued unabated until August, when *U-24* torpedoed the liner *Arabia* off the Irish coast on the 19th. Such was the sharpness of the US protest, although just three American citizens had been among the victims, that the Germans not only ceased to attack passenger liners, but also withdrew their U-boats from western waters.

LEFT: U-boats under construction.

RIGHT: The US liner *Lusitania*, whose sinking in May 1915 caused an outcry in the then neutral United States.

ABOVE: A U-boat tows away the crew of a British steamer which it has just sunk, April 1917.

LEFT: 18 March 1917 – the US tanker *Illinois* sinks in the English Channel, another U-boat victim.

In spite of some losses, U-boat strength grew rapidly during 1915, with over 60 being commissioned. Once again the German Navy pressed for another campaign of unrestricted warfare. In February 1916 another such campaign was announced, but it only really applied to the war zone, with liners not to be touched and only armed vessels to be sunk without warning outside the zone. At the end of March a French passenger liner was torpedoed in the English Channel. Again, US citizens were on board, and fearful that any further such incidents would bring the United States into the war, the German government halted the campaign.

In February 1917 Germany embarked on a policy of totally unrestricted warfare on Allied commerce. The decision-making process which brought it about was complex, but there was a growing realization that the strangling of Britain's sea communications was essential if the war was still to be won. The impact was devastating. With no more than 70 U-boats at sea at any one time, Allied shipping losses rose from just over 100,000 tons in January to over 860,000 tons in April. If Britain was not to starve something had to be done quickly.

Convoying, which history had proved to be the solution, had been used from the outbreak of war, but only for troopships. It was then introduced for the British east coast coal trade in January 1917. The Admiralty resisted using it on a wider scale because of a shortage of escort vessels and doubts over the ability of merchant vessels to maintain station within the convoy. Instead the Royal Navy preferred to patrol the sea lanes. The April losses, however, forced the Admiralty to adopt convoying, encouraged by America's entry into the war since this would make more escorts available.

Convoying took time to implement and was not helped

by initial US Navy resistance to it, but by the autumn it was reaping results. So effective was it that only one percent of ships in convoy fell victim to the U-boats, and the sinkings of these increased. By early 1918 air cover, in the form of fixed-wing aircraft, flying boats and airships, had also been introduced and the U-boats were finding it increasingly difficult to achieve any success. Worse, the loss of U-boats in action was now exceeding the rate of construction.

The Treaty of Versailles forbade Germany to possess submarines or any other type of aggressive weapons. There was also the development in 1918 of a new sub-

marine detection weapon, ASDIC, named after the Allied Submarine Detection Investigation Committee, called SONAR (Sound Navigation and Ranging) by the US Navy. This could detect a submerged submarine through the transmission of a sound impulse which, if it struck a solid object, would rebound in the form of an echo. This was identified with a receiver and the time between transmission and reception could be used to calculate the range. This, together with the success of convoying, appeared to make it unlikely that the submarine would ever be as successful against trade as it had been during 1917. This was reinforced by the 1930

ABOVE: 'We're coming over!' – US troop convoy in mid-Atlantic, May 1918.

RIGHT: A British naval airship escorting a coastal convoy.

LEFT: Germany's only aircraft carrier is launched, 8 December 1938. She was never completed.

BELOW LEFT: The launch of the pocket battleship *Admiral Scheer*.

RIGHT: German naval Commander-in-Chief Erich Raeder.

BELOW RIGHT: A look into the future for a group of naval recruits.

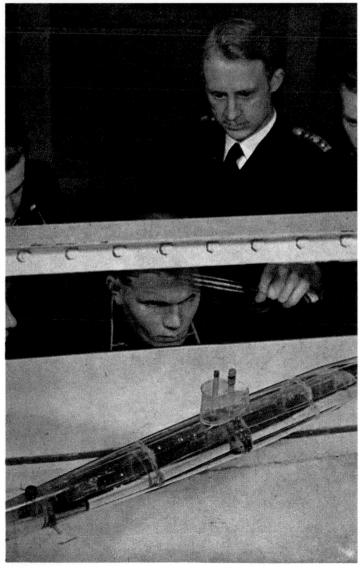

London Naval Treaty signed by all naval powers, including Germany, which reiterated the necessity of ensuring that the crew of a merchant vessel could reach the safety of land or another vessel before their ship was sunk. In view of this, it is hardly surprising that the anti-submarine speciality in the Royal Navy was not given much priority during the years 1919-39 and that very few escorts were built.

When Hitler came to power in 1933 he was keen to throw off the shackles of Versailles and rebuild Germany's armed forces. With regard to the navy he gave priority to the surface fleet, and legality was given to this through the 1935 Anglo-German Naval Treaty, which limited the German surface navy to 35 percent of that of the Royal Navy, but gave her parity in submarines. Hitler assumed that Germany would not find herself at war with Britain again, but at the end of May 1938 he changed his mind. By this time Austria had been annexed and Britain's colder attitude made war a possibility. Germany could only win such a war by matching the Royal Navy and hence Hitler demanded a radical acceleration of the surface ship building program. Plan Z was drawn up, but would not be completed until 1948. While the submarine build was to be increased, priority would remain with surface ships. Most of the senior German naval officers supported this, but one in particular took a different view. Karl Doenitz, himself a World War I submariner, had been appointed to head the U-boat arm in 1935. Remembering how close the U-boats came to bringing Britain to her knees in the spring of 1917, he argued for a production plan based on a massive submarine building program. His was a minority voice. In the meantime, Hitler brushed aside warnings of the danger of going to war with Britain and France before the German Navy was ready.

# OPENING SHOTS

On the evening of 3 September 1939, the day that Britain and France declared war on Germany, the U-boat *U-30* sank the liner SS *Athenia* in the North Atlantic in the mistaken belief that she was an armed merchantman. Among the 112 who lost their lives were 28 US citizens. These were the first fatalities of a campaign that was to last until Germany's final surrender.

In the belief that Hitler had embarked on unrestricted submarine warfare, the British declared a total blockade of Germany and instituted convoying. Although the Admiralty's Trade Division had taken control of all merchant shipping as early as 26 August, convoying took time to organize. Also, because of the severe lack of escort vessels, it was initially only applied to ships with a speed of 9-15 knots. Trans-Atlantic convoys outward bound from Britain were only given a proper escort to a point 100 miles west of Ireland and were then left in the hands of a single armed merchant cruiser for the long voyage across the Atlantic. The U-boats had few successes against ships in convoy during the first months of the war, though. Indeed, up until the end of 1939 only four ships were sunk in convoy as opposed to 102 sailing independently.

As for actively combating the U-boat threat, there were few ASDIC-equipped destroyers available since the bulk were engaged in escorting the British Expeditionary Force and its supplies across the Channel to France, screening duties with the Grand Fleet and protecting the local convoys toiling up and down Britain's east coast. The Admiralty's first plan was therefore to form carrier groups to seek and destroy U-boats in the North Sea. The main weapon used was the World War I 100lb Cooper Bomb, with which Fleet Air Arm and RAF Coastal Command aircraft were equipped. It was not a success. On 5 September an Anson of 233 Squadron, RAF Coastal Command, spotted a submarine on the surface off the west coast of Scotland and attacked it with Cooper Bombs. The submarine, which turned out to be British, submerged and escaped with a shaking, but the bombs had skipped into the air and, as the time fuzes were initiated through impact, the shrapnel from them hit the aircraft, holing its fuel tanks, and it had to put down in the sea. Worse was to happen on the 14th. On this day the first of the seek and destroy groups, built round the carrier HMS *Ark Royal,* had its initial brush with the U-boats. After the carrier herself suffered a near miss from a torpedo, two of her Supermarine Skuas took off and attacked the *U-30* with Cooper Bombs. The bombs burst in the air, downing both aircraft, whose pilots then suffered the indignity of being rescued by the very U-boat which they had tried to attack. The same day did, however, bring about the first Royal Navy success when the destroyers *Faulknor, Firedrake* and *Foxhound* sank *U-39* which had attacked *Ark Royal.* Three days later disaster struck when *U-29* sank the carrier *Courageous* and the Admiralty withdrew its aircraft carriers from anti-submarine operations, although the destroyers continued them for some months to come. Successes, however, were few and far between and only six U-boats had been sunk by the end of 1939.

Doenitz's U-boats were not without their own problems during this initial phase of the Battle of the Atlantic. For a start, since only a small number of ocean-going boats were available, no more than nine were on operational patrol at any one time. Given the size of the

PAGES 12-13: The battlecruiser HMS *Renown*. Note the degaussing cable along the top of her hull.

LEFT: Admiral Karl Doenitz (center) who would conduct the U-boat campaign throughout the war.

BELOW LEFT: U-boat crewmen in a jovial mood.

BOTTOM LEFT: The sinking of the aircraft carrier HMS *Courageous*, Britain's first naval disaster of the war.

RIGHT: U-boat in the North Atlantic.

BELOW: After the loss of the *Courageous* the British gave up using aircraft carriers, like the *Ark Royal*, to hunt U-boats.

LEFT: *U-48*, another Type VIIB, takes torpedoes on board at Kiel.

BELOW LEFT: The Type VIIB *U-52* had a range of 6500 nautical miles.

BOTTOM: Scapa Flow prior to th

ABOVE RIGHT: HMS *Royal Oak.* She was launched in 1914.

RIGHT: Germany's first naval hero of the war, Günther Prien.

North Atlantic, this represented little more than a pin-prick. More frustrating was the fact that the G7a and G7e torpedoes with which they were armed were found to have serious defects. Their depth-keeping mechanisms were unreliable and the magnetic proximity fuzes with which many were equipped frequently caused premature detonation of the warhead. Consequently, many torpedoes fired failed to hit their targets. As Doenitz himself later wrote, 'I do not believe that ever in the history of war have men ever been sent against the enemy with such a useless weapon.' Even so, apart from the sinking of the *Courageous*, there was one other dramatic U-boat success during those early months of the war. On the night of 14/15 October Kapitänleutnant Günther Prien carefully steered *U-47* through the anti-submarine defenses of the British Home Fleet's wartime anchorage at Scapa Flow in the Orkney Islands off the northeast coast of Scotland. Most of the Fleet was out, hunting the pocket battleship *Gneisenau*, but among those ships left behind was the old battleship *Royal Oak*. Prien sent her to the bottom with the loss of 883 members of her crew and became a national hero in Germany overnight.

The Germans had, however, two other weapons in their maritime armory. The first of these was the mine. As the autumn wore on an increasing number of ships were mined in the Thames Estuary, and normal minesweeping techniques did not seem to be working. It became clear that the mines were being laid by low-flying aircraft at night. Eventually, on the night of 21/22 November, an aircraft was detected laying these mines and next morning one was recovered, with parachute attached, from the foreshore. It turned out to be a mag-

netic mine, which lay in wait on the sea bottom ready to react to the magnetic signature which any ship with a metal hull had. The counter to this mine was degaussing, the wrapping of electric cable round the ship's hull, which, when connected to a power supply (the ship's generator), canceled out the ship's inherent field. A crash degaussing program was immediately got underway, as well as the production of additional electric cable for the creation of magnetic mine sweeps. Even so, mines were the cause of one-third of the total Allied tonnage sunk in 1939.

The other major threat, and the one which the British initially believed to be the greatest, was that of the surface warship. The German pocket battleships *Deutschland* and *Graf Spee* had already set sail into the Atlantic before the outbreak of war. The German Navy commander-in-chief, Admiral Erich Raeder, wanted to launch a major offensive against enemy merchant shipping before the Allies could adopt suitable countermeasures, but Hitler was at first unwilling. He still hoped to come to terms with Britain and France, and was loath to risk his numerically inferior surface fleet against the might of the Royal Navy. At the end of September he relented, and *Deutschland* and *Graf Spee* were given orders to begin harrying the sea lanes, but were on no account to engage Allied warships. The *Deutschland* had a disappointing cruise, sinking just two merchant vessels before returning to Germany at the beginning of November with machinery problems. The *Graf Spee* proved a different matter and was to concentrate the thoughts of the Admiralty more than anything else during the Phony War.

LEFT: A victim of the German surface threat.

RIGHT: The *Graf Spee* in the halcyon days of peace.

RIGHT: Units of the Kriegsmarine seek out Allied shipping.

On 30 September, three days after her captain, Hans Langsdorff, had been given his orders to begin his attacks, the *Graf Spee* claimed her first victim, the steamship *Clement* off the Brazilian coast. During the next three weeks she sank a further four ships and then moved into the Indian Ocean. The Admiralty, believing that its entire maritime communications in the South Atlantic were gravely threatened, began to organize task forces to hunt down the *Graf Spee*. No less than seven of these were created, from as far north as Britain (a force built round the battlecruiser *Repulse* and the aircraft carrier *Furious*) to two, also built round carriers, off West Africa; one from the West Indies Squadron; one, which included the French battleship *Strasbourg*, off the Brazilian north coast; down to one from Cape Town; and the last, Force G, made up of four cruisers based on the Falkland Islands. In the meantime, Langsdorff had sunk another British merchantman, off the coast of Mozambique, and stopped a further vessel. Langsdorff now decided to return to the South Atlantic, where he believed the pickings to be richer and on 3 December sank yet another ship, this time off the west coast of South Africa. The *Graf Spee* now moved westward to concentrate on the South America shipping routes, claiming yet another victim on the 7th.

On 21 November, however, the Admiralty was faced with another threat when the battlecruisers *Scharnhost* and *Gneisenau* set sail from Wilhelmshaven to attack the sea routes in the North Atlantic. Two days later, between Iceland and the Faroe Islands, they intercepted a convoy protected by a single armed merchant cruiser, the *Rawalpindi*. Placing herself between the convoy and its attackers, she managed to keep them at bay for long enough to be able to radio a message to the Admiralty and to enable the merchant ships to escape before being sunk by *Scharnhorst*'s guns. The two German ships turned east and the Home Fleet set sail from Scapa to try and intercept them. This failed, and the *Scharnhorst* and *Gneisenau* slipped back into Wilhelmshaven on 27 November.

Back in the South Atlantic, the cruisers of Force G, less the *Cumberland*, which had to put into the Falklands for repairs, had correctly deduced, from radio messages from some of *Graf Spee*'s victims, that Langsdorff was heading for the South American coast and steamed north to the River Plate. On 13 December Langsdorff spotted their smoke and, thinking that they were merely destroyers escorting a convoy, decided to attack. He realized his error too late and found himself with a fierce fight on his hands. While the *Graf Spee*'s heavier armament was able to inflict severe damage on the *Exeter* and *Ajax*, *Achilles* escaped unscathed. Worse, *Graf Spee* herself had been sufficiently damaged to cause Langsdorff to put into Montevideo to carry out repairs before beginning the long voyage back to Germany. Force G remained at the entrance to the Plate estuary and, with the connivance of the British naval attaché at Buenos Aires, managed to bluff Langsdorff into believing that they had been heavily reinforced and that there was no escape for his ship. Therefore, on 17 December, he gave orders for the *Graf Spee* to be scuttled. A few days later he committed suicide in a Buenos Aires hotel bedroom, probably because he could not face the indignity of a court-martial for having disobeyed orders by engaging British warships.

The destruction of the *Graf Spee* gave the British people a much-needed tonic at a time when little appeared to be happening and much of what action there was provided gloomy news. By now, though, the winter gales in the Atlantic were at their height, making life more difficult for both hunter and quarry. Even so, there was no reduction in sinkings; and Hitler's warning

LEFT: A *Graf Spee* victim — SS *Ashlea* was sunk north of St Helena, 7 October 1939.

ABOVE RIGHT: HMS *Exeter* puts into Port Stanley in the Falklands to have her wounds tended after the Battle of the River Plate.

RIGHT: The end of the *Graf Spee*.

LEFT: A British convoy in early 1940. Convoys were very weakly protected at this time.

RIGHT: Wrecked German merchant vessels in a Norwegian harbor, April 1940.

BELOW: The end of a tanker.

BELOW RIGHT: HMS *Cossack* (second from left) bombarding shore batteries, Narvik, 15 April 1940.

of 24 November to neutral shipping to stay away from Allied coasts, and U-boats being allowed to attack any ship not showing lights, meant that they now had more targets than before.

In March 1940 there was, however, a lull in the battle. The reason was Norway. She was neutral, but both the Germans and the Allies recognized her important geo-strategic position. The Allies both wanted to use Norway to transport troops and supplies to help Finland in her struggle against Russia and to prevent the Swedish export of iron ore to Germany, which used the north Norwegian port of Narvik during the winter months. The Germans, recognizing the dangers of an Allied presence in Norway, had already begun to draw up invasion plans in October 1939. Matters were exacerbated in February 1940, when the British destroyer *Cossack* stole into the Jossing fjord and rescued crew members of *Graf Spee*'s victims, who were imprisoned there in the German ship *Altmark*. The lack of positive Norwegian reaction to this confirmed German suspicions that they would not put up much resistance to invasion. In March, the Finns were forced to give up their unequal struggle against the Russians and cede for peace, and this meant that the justification for an Allied invasion of Norway was removed. Nevertheless, the problem of Swedish iron ore remained and it was decided to mine the Norwegian coast instead. Sensing the Allied plan, Hitler gave orders for the invasion of Norway and Denmark at the beginning of April and on the 9th this took place. The invasion fleet was spotted by RAF aircraft on the 7th and British warships were sent to intercept it. During the next week there were a number of naval clashes, notably in the Narvik fjord, and the cost to both sides was high, although it would have been much worse for the British if the U-boat torpedoes had not been so prone to mechanical failure. It was this that finally forced the Germans to do something about their torpedoes. The Allies then landed troops at various places on the Norwegian coast in an effort to

stem the German advance, but they were too ill-coordinated and poorly equipped to be able to do this and at the beginning of June the final evacuations took place, leaving the country in German hands.

From 10 May 1940, however, Norway had been relegated to a sideshow. On that day the long awaited German invasion of France and the Low Countries took place, and the resultant German success would have a significant effect on the Battle of the Atlantic.

# THE FIRST HAPPY TIME

H32

The surrender of France in June 1940 left Britain in a grievous plight. Not only was she now bereft of allies, but invasion seemed imminent. Furthermore she now had another enemy, in that Mussolini had finally declared war. Besieged as Britain was, her maritime lifelines were now even more vital, but they had suddenly come under even greater threat. For a start, the Royal Navy's high losses of ships during the Norwegian campaign and, more especially, during the evacuation of the BEF from Dunkirk meant that the shortage of convoy escort vessels was still as severe as ever. Matters were made worse by the presence of a large hostile fleet in the Mediterranean. Merchant ships could no longer risk using this route to India and the Far East and had to take the longer Cape route round South Africa. It also meant that the British Mediterranean Fleet could not now be used to reinforce the Atlantic.

Perhaps the most significant event was that the Germans now had the use of the French Atlantic coast bases. Transferring the U-boats to these saved them an often hazardous 450-mile passage through the North Sea into the Atlantic and meant that more could be on operational patrol at any one time. The first of these bases, Lorient, became operational on 6 July, and this was quickly followed by the others at Bordeaux, Brest, La Pallice (La Rochelle), and St Nazaire. In order to solve the torpedo problem, the magnetic proximity fuze was removed and only the more reliable impact fuzes used, and the torpedoes were set to run shallow so as to minimize the variations in depth-keeping. Meanwhile greater priority was given to the development of new and more effective torpedoes. One new weapon was introduced. A wing of long-range Focke Wulf FW200 Kondor aircraft was deployed to the French Atlantic coast. The main role of these was to locate convoys for the U-boats, but they would also be used as U-boat radio beacons and to attack shipping on their own – indeed, they sank no less than 30 ships during their first two months of operations. Doenitz set up his headquarters in Paris, and, in order to produce a stranglehold on Britain, Hitler declared a total maritime blockade on 17 August, stating that neutral shipping would be sunk without warning.

At this time the German priority was to achieve the right conditions over the English Channel and southern England for a successful amphibious invasion. Crucial to this was the gaining of air superiority and at the time of Hitler's total blockade declaration the Battle of Britain was reaching a climax. One early result of it, however, was that losses through air action meant that it was no longer possible for shipping to use the Channel and it had to be diverted through the North Channel between Scotland and Ireland. This acted like a bottleneck and provided a good target concentration for the U-boats. A further problem was that almost from the outbreak of war the German radio intercept service, the *B Dienst (Beobachter Dienst* or Monitor Service), had been able to read the British & Allied Merchant Ship (BAMS) code and this sometimes enabled U-boats to locate a convoy.

PAGES 24-25: British shipping losses during the evacuation from Dunkirk aggravated convoy escort problems. The destroyer HMS *Havant* was one of the victims.

RIGHT: Concrete U-boat pens at St Nazaire, one of the main French U-boat bases. These pens successfully withstood all attempts to bomb them from the air.

BELOW: Another desperately needed tanker-load of oil fails to get through to Britain.

BELOW LEFT: The scourge of the Atlantic – the Focke Wulf FW200 Kondor had a range of 2200 miles.

ABOVE: British troops being evacuated from France.

LEFT: Another convoy braves the Atlantic.

ABOVE RIGHT: *U-74*, a Type VIIB, was commissioned in 1940. In September 1941 she sank the Canadian corvette *Levis*.

RIGHT CENTER: Another torpedoed tanker heads to the bottom, November 1940.

RIGHT: *U-124*'s torpedo compartment.

The convoys themselves were now organized into four types. Fast inward convoys (9-14.9 knots) assembled at Halifax, Nova Scotia, had the prefix HX. Slow inward convoys (SC – 7.5-9 knots) assembled at Sydney, Cape Breton. Outward convoys were not dependent on speed, but were classified as OA (those assembling on the British east coast) and OB (assembling elsewhere in British waters). Throughout most of their passage across the Atlantic the convoys still had just one escort vessel, and it was only the area from the south of Iceland to British ports that more escort vessels joined, together with RAF Coastal Command air cover. Even so, during the period July 1940-April 1941, which the U-boat crews termed the 'First Happy Time,' it was in this area that most of the sinkings took place. The reason for this was that the escorts themselves, old sloops and Flower Class corvettes, lacked the technical means to be able to deal with the U-boats.

In order to both minimize the torpedo depth-keeping problem and to make maximum use of speed, the U-boats took to making surface attacks by night. The Type VIIB and VIIC U-boats had a maximum surface speed of 17 knots (underwater speed was a mere 7.5-8 knots). Since a convoy was governed by the speed of the slowest ship it was easy for the U-boats to catch it up and make good their escape after they had attacked, especially since the escorts themselves could barely do 15 knots. Worse, they had no means, apart from visual, of

detecting a U-boat on the surface and no coherent tactics for hunting a U-boat once it had attacked. Given all these facts, it is hardly surprising that the U-boats enjoyed some spectacular successes. Typical of these successes were the attacks against Convoy SC7, which lost 20 ships sunk and two damaged out of a total of 34, in October 1940. Indeed, the monthly shipping losses for September and October 1940 rose to over 400,000 tons, twice what the average monthly loss had been during the previous autumn and winter. Only bad weather in November reduced the sinkings.

Desperate measures were needed to rectify the chronic shortage of escorts. Prime Minister Churchill approached President Roosevelt and offered a deal. In return for a 90-year lease on British naval bases in the Caribbean, Roosevelt presented 50 vintage World War I destroyers to the Royal Navy. The US Congress approved this measure on 2 September and four days later the first six 'four-stackers' were handed over. Their sea-keeping qualities were doubtful, but they were better than nothing to fill the gap until sufficient modern escort vessels were available.

If November 1940 saw a lull in U-boat activity, it also brought about a resurgence of the surface threat. On the 5th the pocket battleship *Admiral Scheer* contacted Convoy HX84 south of Greenland. Escorted by the armed merchant cruiser *Jervis Bay*, it was a mirror action to that of Captain Kennedy (father of Ludovic Kennedy, the well-known broadcaster) in the *Rawalpindi* the previous year. *Jervis Bay* held off her adver-

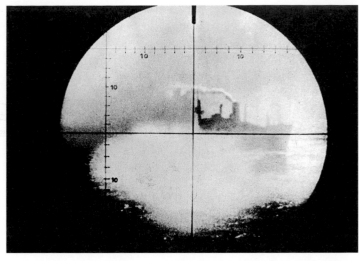

ABOVE, FAR LEFT: A U-boat in mid-Atlantic.

ABOVE LEFT: A submariner in action.

LEFT: HMS *Azalea*, a Flower class corvette, 1940.

ABOVE RIGHT (both): 'Fire one!' – the view of the target through the periscope and the moment of torpedo impact.

RIGHT: The US 'four-stackers' (in foreground) which helped ease the desperate shortage of escort vessels in the fall of 1940.

sary while the convoy scattered before being sunk. This time *Admiral Scheer* managed to sink four other ships from the convoy and then steamed down to the South Atlantic, accounting for a further 15 ships before returning home. On 7 December another major surface raider left Kiel on an anti-convoy cruise. This was the heavy cruiser *Admiral Hipper*, which had been badly damaged at the outset of the Norwegian campaign when she had been rammed by the destroyer *Glowworm*. On Christmas Eve she came across a troop convoy, WS5A, bound for the Middle East. These convoys had high priority since this was the only land theater in which British and Dominion land forces were actively engaged against the enemy. Hence, they had a much stronger escort, which, in this case, included the heavy cruiser *Berwick*, two light cruisers, and two elderly aircraft carriers, *Argus* and *Furious*. *Admiral Hipper* managed to damage two troopships before she was seen off by this strong escort, which damaged her. She subsequently sank one independent vessel before putting into Brest on 27 December, the first major German surface ship to dock at a French Atlantic port in the war.

In the new year the surface threat continued to trouble the Admiralty. The *Admiral Hipper*, her damage repaired, slipped out of Brest on 1 February 1941. Eleven days later she got in among an unescorted convoy bound from Freetown in West Africa, destroying seven out of 19 ships before returning to Brest. On 4 February, after having been foiled once by the British Home Fleet, the *Scharnhorst* and *Gneisenau* managed to get out of the Baltic and into the Atlantic. They created havoc in the shipping lanes, sending 115,000 tons of shipping to the bottom of the ocean before putting into Brest on 22 March. Shipping losses during the month of February 1941 approached 400,000 tons again, but there were some glimmers of hope for the British.

Firstly, thanks to the US destroyer loan and also because the threat of invasion had been receding, more escorts were becoming available and the escort limit could now be extended farther westward. The escorts themselves began to be fitted with a radar device, the 1.4m ASV Mk 2, which could detect a U-boat on the surface, albeit only out to a range of three miles. RAF Coastal Command also began to be more effective. Through Lend-Lease it began to receive the Consolidated Catalina (called the Canso by the Canadians) flying boat. Its 3000-mile range and excellent observation facilities made it an ideal long-range maritime patrol aircraft. The useless anti-submarine bomb was discarded in favor of the depth charge and, for sake of unity of command, RAF Coastal Command was put under the operational control of the Admiralty in order to fight the Battle of the Atlantic. The naval focus for the battle was HQ Western Approaches, which was moved from Plymouth to the more central position of Liverpool and No 15 Group, RAF Coastal Command, located with it. In spring 1941 Coastal Command aircraft and escorts were sent to Iceland and convoys rerouted north to take advantage of this additional scope for protection. There was, too, a major overhaul of anti-submarine training, and the center for this was moved from Portland on the Dorset coast to the River Clyde in Scotland, and escorts were given a month's work-up training before they became operational. Finally, the Admiralty was beginning to obtain better information on U-boat movements. As yet, the ability to decipher the U-boat Enigma codes in which they transmitted their messages was slight, but shore-based listening stations using High Frequency Direction Finding equipment, or Huff Duff as it was commonly known, could pinpoint U-boat positions from

ABOVE: The *Admiral Hipper*.

LEFT: The *Jervis Bay* which fought an unequal battle against the *Admiral Sheer*. Her captain, Fogarty Fegen, was awarded a posthumous Victoria Cross.

RIGHT: The aircraft carrier *Argus*, completed in 1918, which helped to see off the *Admiral Hipper* in December 1940.

their radio transmissions. From this information the Admiralty's Submarine Tracking Room could sometimes deduce where likely U-boat concentrations were and reroute convoys accordingly.

The result of these improvements began to make itself felt in March 1941. The U-boats themselves were beginning to hunt in groups, known as 'wolf packs.' One of these attacked Convoy OB293 south of Iceland. After sinking two ships and damaging two others the U-boats were attacked by the escort, which sank one and damaged another. Most of the boats then made off, except for *U-47* of *Royal Oak* fame, which continued to harry the convoy, but was then sunk by the destroyer *Wolverine* and lost with all hands, including Prien. The remainder of the pack located another convoy, this time a homeward one, but it had a strong escort of five destroyers and two corvettes. The convoy lost six ships, but *U-100* was rammed and sunk by *Vanoc*. Furthermore, *U-99*, skippered by the top-scoring ace Otto Kretschmer, was so badly damaged that it was forced to surrender to *Vanoc* and *Walker*. The loss of three U-boat aces (Schepke of *U-100* was also one) in such a short period was a bad blow to Doenitz and he was forced to deploy his boats deeper into the Atlantic. The 'First Happy Time' was coming to an end.

The final nail in the coffin came in May. The Royal Canadian Navy (RCN), which at the outbreak of war had possessed just seven destroyers and five minesweepers, had been expanding rapidly. Through its newly formed Newfoundland Escort Group it was now able to escort convoys as far east as 35°W. Here, at the Mid-Ocean Meeting Point (MOMP), Iceland-based escorts took over and, in their turn, handed over to Western Approaches escorts at 18°W. Thus, convoys could now be given a proper escort throughout the crossing. It would, however, be some time before one continuous escort could be provided because of a lack of facilities for refueling at sea, an essential prerequisite given the limited range of the escorts.

May 1941, too, saw a dramatic development in the intelligence battle. In a clash with Convoy OB318 seven U-boats managed to sink nine vessels and damage two others, but during this *U-110* was damaged and surrendered. She was taken under tow, but sank, but this was not before a boarding party had seized her Enigma cipher machine and codebooks. Earlier, on 27 February, the British had managed to obtain a set of spare Enigma

rotors from the captured trawler *Krebs* during the commando raid on the Lofoten Islands, but now they had the machine itself and were able to decipher the U-boat Enigma traffic in as little as 24 hours after the transmission of messages. This made them privy to Doenitz's operational plans and many more convoys could now be diverted to avoid the wolf packs. The effects of this and the escort improvements were graphically demonstrated in the number of merchant ships sunk. During the quarter April-June 1941 no less than 150 ships were sunk in the Atlantic, but this fell away to 90 during the next quarter and 70 for the last quarter of the year. This was at a time when the number of operational U-boats was steadily increasing. Gradually the Germans came to realize that somehow the British were obtaining information sufficient for them to reroute convoys, but they refused to believe that it was penetration of Enigma which was the cause.

During the early summer Doenitz switched his priority to convoys off the West African seaboard, where convoy discipline was more lax than in the North Atlantic. In May alone the U-boats sank 30 ships, but more escorts were then provided and the rate of sinkings fell away. Another reason for this was attributable to Ultra, which became the generic codeword for the reading of the Enigma traffic. In order to keep his U-boats longer on patrol and hence have more in the Atlantic at any one time Doenitz had organized a number of merchant ships to resupply the U-boats at sea. Ultra quickly located all these during the summer and they were destroyed one by one.

Yet, if the U-boat threat was becoming slightly less grievous that of the surface ship still remained. A stark reminder of this occurred also in May 1941. On the 18th the battleship *Bismarck* and heavy cruiser *Prinz Eugen* left the Polish port of Gydnia (now Gdansk) for an Atlantic cruise. Three days later RAF reconnaissance

ABOVE LEFT: U-boats setting out for rich pickings in the Atlantic.

BELOW LEFT: Otto Kretschmer, top U-boat ace of the 'First Happy Time.' He rose to admiral's rank in the postwar German Navy.

ABOVE: U-boat maintenance check in mid-Atlantic.

ABOVE RIGHT: A submariner is welcomed back to port after a successful cruise.

RIGHT CENTER: Some of the crew of the destroyer *Vanoc* which sank the ace Jürgen Schepke in *U-100*.

RIGHT: *Bismarck* seen from the *Prinz Eugen*.

aircraft spotted them in the Norwegian harbor of Bergen and the Home Fleet was alerted. On the 23rd they were sighted in the Denmark Strait and the Home Fleet moved to intercept them. Next day they were contacted and engaged by the battleships *Hood* and *Prince of Wales*. It was a disaster. The *Hood*, the Royal Navy's pride and joy for many years, was hit and blew up with the loss of all but three of her crew, while the *Prince of Wales* was damaged. The two German ships then separated and were lost from view. Churchill himself gave an order that the *Bismarck* must be found and sunk at all cost and units of the Mediterranean Fleet were ordered into the Atlantic. On the 26th an RAF Coastal Command Catalina spotted the *Bismarck* 700 miles west of Brest and that evening a Swordfish torpedo strike from *Ark Royal* damaged her steering gear, forcing her to reduce speed. Next day the battleships *King George V* and *Rodney* caught up with her and in an unequal duel she was finally sunk, with only 110 survivors. *Prinz Eugen*, on the other hand, managed to elude her hunters and slipped into Brest on 1 June. The saga illustrated how very sensitive to the surface threat the planners at the Admiralty still were.

It was becoming increasingly recognized that air power had a vital part to play in the protection of Allied shipping in the Atlantic. Although the introduction of the Catalina had helped increase RAF Coastal Command's coverage, as well as that of the Royal Canadian Air Force (RCAF), there was still a very significant gap in the mid-Atlantic. Known as the 'Black Gap,' this could only be filled with very long-range maritime patrol aircraft. Matters were not helped by the fact that deliveries of the Catalina were slow. Four-engined aircraft were what were really needed, but the Air Ministry resisted any diversion in the production of heavy bombers since it saw its priority as developing the strategic bombing

offensive against Germany. There was another aircraft which would fit the bill, the US Consolidated Liberator, and a squadron's worth was procured in spring 1941 for Coastal Command, but they initially suffered from mechanical problems and were virtually non-operational. Meanwhile the 'Black Gap' remained.

Another concern was the activities of the Focke Wulf Kondors, which had proved to be very successful in drawing the U-boats on to convoys as well as sinking ships themselves. The answer to this was the Fighter Catapult Ship. This was a merchant vessel converted to carry a single Hawker Hurricane fighter, which was literally catapulted off the deck and, at the end of its sortie, it ditched into the sea and the pilot was hopefully retrieved. Four of these were ready in April 1941 and the first success came on 2 August when a Hurricane launched from HMS *Maplin* shot down a Kondor which was threatening Convoy SC81. These ships were Royal Navy, but in their wake came 50 CAM-ships (Catapult Armed Merchantman), normal merchant vessels with the pilot and aircraft carried as supernumaries.

Another worrying fact was that it had been noticed at the beginning of the year that the Germans were starting to construct massive concrete shelters or pens in which to house their U-boats in the French Atlantic ports. Coastal Command wanted Bomber Command to attack them, but the latter merely viewed this as an unnecessary diversion from their saturation attacks on Germany *per se*.

The summer of 1941 also witnessed growing US involvement in the Battle of the Atlantic. The passing of the Lend-Lease Bill by Congress in March 1941 triggered an enormous increase in shipping from the USA to Britain. Concerned that US merchant ships should not become U-boat fodder, Roosevelt declared on 11 April that the Pan-American security zone in the Atlantic was

LEFT: Hunting the *Bismarck*, May 1941. Swordfish aircraft standby on the deck of HMS *Victorious*.

ABOVE RIGHT: A CAM ship with Hurricane on deck.

RIGHT: The battle of 24 May 1941. A shell from HMS *Hood* lands some way from the *Bismarck*. The photograph was taken from *Prinz Eugen*.

ABOVE: Newly arrived US troops pictured in Iceland. Taking over the garrison of this vital island was one of the escalatory steps in the US involvement in the Battle of the Atlantic.

LEFT: A Lend-Lease convoy to Russia comes under attack.

RIGHT: The crippled USS *Kearney* just after her arrival at Reykjavik, Iceland.

extended from 60°W to 26°W. The US Navy would take every measure to protect US ships within this zone. Not wishing to confront the USA, Hitler ordered the U-boats to stay out of the zone. In that same month US troops established bases in Greenland and these would soon play an important role in the battle. This was followed in July by the relief of the British garrison on Iceland by US troops. This meant that the US Navy now had justification to escort convoys as far as the island and it also marked another escalation in US involvement.

Matters took another step forward in August when Churchill sailed in *Prince of Wales* for his first face-to-face meeting with Roosevelt, which took place in Placentia Bay, Newfoundland. Although he failed in his main object to persuade Roosevelt to join in the war against the Axis powers he did obtain Roosevelt's agreement to increased participation in the Battle of the Atlantic. US warships would now escort vessels not flying the American flag and the MOMP was shifted to 22°W, which meant that the Western Approaches escort groups could now return direct to their home ports after handing over outward convoys, rather than having to put into Iceland to refuel. US and British naval staffs would work out escort details for each convoy jointly, although the organization of the convoy system as a whole remained with the British.

It was now inevitable that sooner or later there would be clashes between US warships and U-boats, in spite of Hitler's edict that the US Navy should be left well alone. The first of these occurred on 17 October when the destroyer USS *Kearney* was torpedoed by a U-boat northwest of Iceland. Although badly damaged, she was able to

limp into port. Two weeks later, on the 31st, another destroyer, USS *Reuben James,* was sunk by *U-552.* As provocative as these actions might appear, they were still not enough to persuade the American people that they must declare war.

In the meantime, the increasing number of U-boats coming off the slipways meant that Doenitz could now form larger wolf packs. The first of these was formed in August 1941 in the North Atlantic between Greenland and Iceland and consisted of some 15 boats. In September they had a major success, attacking Convoy SC42 and sinking 16 ships, and this in spite of rerouting as a result of Ultra intercepts. During the autumn Doenitz deployed four more groups in the same area. These swept east to west, but did not enjoy the same success. Before Doenitz could develop these new tactics any further he was ordered by Hitler to send some of his boats to the Mediterranean to give support to Rommel in North Africa. Other boats were to go to Norway. The reasons for this were twofold. Firstly, Hitler feared that the British were preparing a major operation against Norway. Furthermore, in an effort to give support to the Russians, who were under intense pressure from the German invasion which was now threatening Moscow, Churchill had begun to send convoys of weapons and raw materials to the northern ports of Murmansk and Archangel. The first of these, PQ1, had set sail on 26 September, and a further six convoys were sent by the end of the year. All managed to get through without loss. These redeployments drastically restricted Doenitz's operations in the Atlantic, but before the year was out there was to be a dramatic development.

# THE SECOND HAPPY TIME

On 7 December 1941 the Japanese attacked Pearl Harbor and the USA found herself at war with Japan. Roosevelt was, however, in a dilemma since he was not confident that the US people would consider an additional declaration of war against Germany and Italy as justified. In the event, his difficulty was overcome for him by Hitler, who, together with Mussolini, declared war on the United States on 11 December. Two days before this, however, Hitler had lifted his ban on U-boats operating in the Pan-American security zone.

Doenitz had had his eye on the US eastern seaboard for some time and wanted to immediately deploy 12 of his new Type IX ocean-going boats to this area. The Mediterranean and Norwegian requirements meant that he could only initially send five. The attraction of the eastern seaboard was the large amount of shipping which plied up and down it. On 1 July 1941, in an effort to organize protection for this traffic, the coast had been split into a number of 'sea frontiers.' These were responsible for providing sea and air protection up to 200 miles from the coast. On 1 November the US Navy had taken over control of the Coast Guard and its vessels, but there was still a desperate shortage of escort ships and the Coast Guard cutters were singularly ill-equipped for anti-submarine operations. Hence it was considered impracticable to attempt to institute convoying and instead, on 7 December, all merchant vessels were ordered to follow designated coast-hugging routes so as to take maximum advantage of the limited air cover available. Unfortunately, no attempt was made to institute any form of black-out on the coast and lights continued to shine as they had before war had been declared. No wonder that Doenitz and his U-boat skippers were keen to begin operations there.

On 12 January 1942 came the first success in Doenitz's offensive in US waters, which he codenamed Operation *Paukenschlag* (Drumroll), when *U-123* sank the British steamer *Cyclops* 300 miles east of Cape Cod. She was the first of 46 ships sunk that month, of which all but six were off the eastern seaboard. The lack of anti-submarine vessels and convoying and the bright backcloth of the coast, which made targets only too easy to identify by night, provided perfect conditions for the U-boats and it is hardly surprising that their crews would call this the 'Second Happy Time.'

From the point of view of the Allies, the Atlantic had now increased even more in importance. During the last part of December and first two weeks of January they had held the first of their major wartime conferences, at Washington DC, codenamed Arcadia. The prime decision to come out of this was that the defeat of Germany would take priority over that of Japan. In pursuit of this the Americans were to build up their military strength in Britain (codename Bolero) and an operation against the continent of Europe in 1942 was planned in order to relieve the pressure on the Russians. The sea lanes therefore had to be made as secure as possible for Bolero to be successfully achieved.

Thanks to Drumroll, the North Atlantic saw a significant fall in sinkings in January 1942. There were also a number of further improvements, technical and otherwise, in the fight against the U-boats, which were being

PAGES 40-41: One of the workhorses of the Battle of the Atlantic, the Flower class corvette HMS *Bluebell.*

LEFT: A victim of 'Drumroll,' the US tanker *Dixie Arrow* was torpedoed off Cape Hatteras, 26 March 1942.

ABOVE RIGHT: The crew of *U-123*, a Type IXB ocean-going boat, prepare to engage a merchant vessel with their 37mm flak gun.

RIGHT: The British destroyer *Skate* setting off a depth charge during a U-boat hunt.

introduced. Huff Duff began to be fitted to escorts, giving them another means of locating U-boats. Their 1.5m radars were also being replaced by a 10cm version with a range of four miles. They were also being given the American Talk Between Ships (TBS) system, which provided a means of secure communications. There was also a new anti-submarine weapon, Hedgehog. This was a system which fired a number of bombs simultaneously over the bows, rather than astern as with the conventional depth charge, and hence was much more responsive to ASDIC contacts. The policy now was to try and organize permanent escort groups, whose ships worked with each other the whole time. In this context, in January 1942 Western Approaches set up the Western Approaches Tactical Unit (WATU) at its headquarters at Derby House, Liverpool. This carried out a detailed analysis of U-boat tactics and during 1942 evolved a number of standard escort search and attack drills, named after types of fruit. WATU also ran six-day courses for escort captains and many attended more than one.

All these measures boded well for the future, but on 1 February the Allies suffered a serious blow – they could no longer read Ultra. Up until then the U-boats had been using the Hydra Enigma cipher, the same as was used by all surface ships in the Baltic and North Sea. Now a dedicated U-boat cipher, Triton, came into force. This was to defy the efforts of Bletchley Park, the British Code and Cipher School, to crack it until almost the end of the year. Bletchley Park was still able to decipher Hydra and continued to gain much valuable U-boat intelligence from it, but the task of the Submarine Tracking Room

was now much harder than it had been.

Meanwhile, the toll of sinkings off the eastern seaboard increased during February. On the 16th Doenitz ordered a mass U-boat attack and the total number of victims for the month was 71, with again all but six in US waters. Even worse was the fact that not a single U-boat had yet been sunk by US forces. This was rectified, however, on the first day of March, when a Hudson from Squadron VP-82 based at Argentia, Newfoundland, sank *U-656*, a Type VIIC, off Cape Race, Newfoundland. Two weeks later came the next success, again to a VP-82 Hudson. Not until the night of 13/14 April would a US warship sink a U-boat, when USS *Roper* despatched *U-85* south of Norfolk, Virginia. March, however, saw the sinkings increase even further, with 86 ships being sunk in US waters. What was especially serious about this figure was that more than half were tankers. Furthermore, the sinkings in the Atlantic for March represented a total of 562,336 tons, greater than any month since the beginning of the war.

Indeed, it was a dark time for the Allies, with the Japanese sweeping all before them in the Pacific and Rommel having forced the British back to the Gazala Line in Libya. Another event, in February 1942, also did little to inspire hope. The surface threat to the Atlantic remained in the shape of the *Scharnhorst*, *Gneisenau* and *Prinz Eugen*, which had been in port at Brest since the previous spring. RAF Bomber Command had made a number of attacks on them, but with little success. Nevertheless, the Germans considered that they were too vulnerable and in mid-January, Admiral Otto Ciliax, commanding the squadron, was given orders to sail it to home ports. He decided that the best way to avoid the

British Home Fleet would be to sail straight up the English Channel and into the North Sea. Accordingly, on the evening of 11 February the ships slipped anchor. Not until the mid-morning of the next day did the British realize that they were on the move. By this time Ciliax was entering the Straits of Dover. An attack made by Motor Torpedo Boats (MTBs) was unsuccessful. This was followed by a virtually suicidal attack by six Fleet Air Arm Swordfish operating at their extreme range. All but one were shot down and their torpedoes missed. In the afternoon *Scharnhorst* was slightly damaged by a mine, but further attacks by Harwich-based destroyers and aircraft of both RAF Bomber and Coastal Commands were as fruitless as the earlier ones. On the 13th Ciliax's ships arrived in triumph at the North Sea ports of Wilhelmshaven and Brunsbuttel. They had coolly walked through Britain's 'front garden' and got away with it. The only consolation for the British came before the month was out when the submarine HMS *Trident* torpedoed *Prinz Eugen* on her way to Norway, putting her out of action until May, and a bomber attack on the night of 26/27 February caused sufficient damage to *Gneisenau* to prevent her from ever putting to sea again under her own power.

The American naval commander-in-chief at this time was Admiral Ernest J King, who had until just before Christmas 1941 commanded the US Atlantic Fleet. While he believed, like the vast majority of senior US naval officers, that the Allied priority should be the defeat of Japan and that the bulk of US naval assets should be concentrated to this end, he did recognize the vital importance of winning the Battle of the Atlantic. Indeed, he took personal control of it from the American side and proposed that the Americans take over responsibility for the northwest Atlantic. This was agreed by the British and came into effect in March 1942. King set up Task Force 24 to control all ocean escort groups in this area,

with the RCN-controlled Western Local Escort Force, responsible for feeder convoys, also being placed under its command. The changeover point between British and US control in the North Atlantic was established as 26°W and this was known as the CHOP (Change of Operational Control) Line. This step helped to rationalize the Allied operational organization in the North Atlantic, but the problem of the American eastern seaboard continued to be severe.

It was not until 1 April, three months after the opening of Drumroll, that any form of convoying was instituted and then it was only partial. Shipping now formed convoys which, hugging the coast, were escorted by day. At night they anchored in protected harbors. These convoys were known as the 'Bucket Brigade.' It was a step in the right direction but, even so, did not apply to the Caribbean or the Gulf of Mexico. Later that month the local civil authorities were finally persuaded to dowse all lights on the coast. Their reason for refusing to do so up until then was that it would adversely affect the tourist trade! This measure did slightly reduce the sinkings that month, but the U-boats themselves began to move into the still largely undefended Caribbean. A further development that month was the despatch from Germany of a new type of U-boat, the Type XIV *Milchkuh* (Milk Cow). This carried some 600 tons of additional fuel, together with spare torpedoes and other supplies and meant that Doenitz once more had a means of keeping his U-boats supplied at sea.

Partially thanks to the arrival of the Type XIVs the Germans were able to concentrate 32 U-boats off the eastern seaboard and in the Caribbean in May. The result of this was that sinkings increased to 111 ships, representing nearly 650,000 tons, in May and climbed to 121 in June. This equated to 652,487 tons and was the most expensive month in the Atlantic for the Allies during the whole war. Local convoys were now implemented in the

LEFT: When on the surface it was imperative that U-boat crews remained alert at all times, especially in view of the growing air threat.

RIGHT: The pocket battleship *Lützow* (formerly *Deutschland*), was one of the major threats to Arctic convoys during 1942.

Caribbean and Gulf of Mexico, but it was not until 1 August, when the Interlocking Convoy System was introduced, that comprehensive convoy protection was instituted. The 'Second Happy Time' came to an end and Doenitz turned once more to the North Atlantic.

It had been recognized for more than a year that there were other methods of keeping the U-boats at bay apart from during convoy battles. One of these was to attack the sources of U-boat production. The ebullient 'Bomber' Harris, who took over RAF Bomber Command in February 1942 had, however, been given a directive which stated that his prime aim was to be 'focused on the morale of the enemy civil population and in particular that of the industrial workers.' He interpreted this as 'city busting,' but argued that his bomber strength was as yet too low. If it was radically increased he believed that he could bring Germany to her knees, but to attack specific industrial targets would merely be a diversion from this. He was supported in this by Portal, Chief of the Air Staff. Consequently Coastal Command remained the 'poor relation' both in terms of aircraft production and technical aids. As a sop Coastal Command did, however, receive a number of elderly Whitleys and Wellingtons. These were to form the backbone of what became known as the Bay Offensive. The U-boats operating from the French Atlantic ports had to traverse the Bay of Biscay in order to reach their operational areas. It thus made sense to make every effort to destroy them there. During 1941 Coastal Command began to concentrate on this task, but it was a frustrating business. Although most aircraft were equipped with the ASV Mk2 radar, its serviceability record was poor, and most sightings of U-boats were visual on the surface. Even so, the U-boat was invariably able to crash dive before an effective attack could be launched on it and dropping depth charges on the spot where it had dived also brought no result. Also, Doenitz ordered his boats to make the Bay

passage by night, which made them even more difficult to spot. Indeed, during the whole of 1941 there was only one successful contact when a Whitley of 502 Squadron located *U-206* by radar and sank it.

During the early part of 1942 means were developed to make Coastal Command more effective. Two of these measures were introduced by operational analysts working for the Command. In order to overcome the problem of the U-boat sighting the aircraft in time enough for it to escape by crash diving, the underside of all Coastal Command aircraft was painted white since this was found to be the color which blended best with the sky. They also recommended that aircraft-delivered depth charges be set to detonate at 25 feet below the surface of the sea as being the optimum depth to catch the diving U-boat. In order to better detect a U-boat on the surface at night a simple device called the Leigh Light was introduced. This was nothing more than a powerful searchlight mounted on the underside of the aircraft, which would be switched on during the final run-in to attack after the U-boat had been identified by radar. Five Leigh Light Wellingtons began to operate in the Bay in June 1942. During June and July they made 11 sightings. Six attacks came from these, which resulted in one U-boat sunk and two damaged. The U-boat crews began to refer to *das verdammte Licht* ('that damned light') and in the middle of July Doenitz countermanded his earlier order. The U-boats would now make the passage by day. During August and September there was a dramatic increase in daylight sightings and some sinkings, although the Luftwaffe's Atlantic Air Command did provide a level of protective cover.

In September the U-boats began to be fitted with a new electronic gadget, Metox. The Germans had captured an ASV radar and from it developed a receiver which could detect it operating from aircraft up to ranges of 30 miles. At the same time they introduced antiaircraft armament for the U-boats. Thus, by the end of 1942 the pendulum had swung their way once more.

By autumn 1942 the focus of attention was drawn once more to the North Atlantic. Doenitz concentrated on developing his wolf pack tactics. Now the packs consisted of some 12-18 boats each. They operated in an extended line with a four-mile interval between boats and would initially sweep westward, looking for a westward-bound convoy. When a U-boat sighted one it would transmit a sighting report to Doenitz's HQ in Paris. The other boats would then be directed on to the convoy. Once in western Atlantic waters, those boats requiring replenishment would rendezvous with a U-boat tanker, usually to the northeast of Bermuda. The boats would then form a new line in the Newfoundland Bank area and sweep eastward to locate an eastward convoy. At the end of this those needing replenishment would return to port, while the remainder formed a fresh pack with new arrivals.

The majority of convoys still managed to get across the Atlantic unscathed, either by skillful routing, or by aircraft and escorts distracting the sighting U-boat before it could guide the others on to the convoy. Nevertheless, when the U-boats did successfully make contact the damage could be severe. Thus, Convoy SC94 lost 11 out of 36 ships in August, although the escorts sank two U-boats, and in September ON127 had eight ships sunk, including a destroyer escort. Indeed, sinkings in the Atlantic did not fall below a monthly tonnage of 500,000

until December, when bad weather inhibited the operations of the U-boats. The Black Gap southwest of Iceland still existed and the majority of sinkings took place in this area. Merchant vessels which, through damage, mechanical fault or simply because they were too slow, fell behind the convoy, the so-called stragglers, were also easy meat. The most serious implication of this high rate of sinkings was that they continued to exceed the rate of new merchant ship construction, and this in spite of the Liberty ship. This represented a new ship-building technique, whereby a ship was constructed of prefabricated sections which could be built far away from the coast. It was only the final stage of assembly that required a proper shipyard by the water and this meant a dramatic increase in building capacity. The first of these ships, the *Patrick Henry*, was launched at the end of September 1941 and it would not be long before Liberty ships dominated the Allied merchant fleet.

In November 1942, so serious did Churchill view the situation in the Atlantic that he formed a special Anti-U-Boat Committee as a sub-committee of the Committee of Imperial Defence. What was clear was that there was still a crucial shortage of escort vessels. Indeed, the First Lord of the Admiralty considered that 1050 were needed, but that there were only 450 available that November. This had to be taken against the fact that the U-boat numerical strength was increasing rapidly. Thus, by December 1942 there were 200 operational where there had only been 90 at the beginning of the year.

LEFT: German submariners prepare to fire their torpedoes.

ABOVE RIGHT: A product of new American shipbuilding techniques – the tanker *Sinclair H-C*, which took only 76 days to construct.

RIGHT: The threat in being – *Tirpitz* in the Narvik-Bogen Fjord, northern Norway, July 1942. Note the anti-submarine nets surrounding her.

The escort problem was aggravated by the need for them in other areas than the North Atlantic. This was especially so with the Russian convoys. By early 1942 the Germans had radically strengthened their anti-shipping forces in Norway. Doenitz had sent additional submarines and the Luftwaffe was also made to send more aircraft. More serious, as it appeared at the time, was that the battleship *Tirpitz* was now positioned here, ready to strike. Two attacks on her by RAF Bomber Command were unsuccessful and the threat that she posed troubled the Admiralty greatly. From March onward the Russian convoys began to suffer increasing losses, especially as the Arctic summer with its perpetual daylight drew on, although not from the *Tirpitz*, which made one just unsuccessful foray against PQ12 in March.

The climax came in July with Convoy PQ17. It was strongly escorted, at least by Atlantic standards. Its 33 merchantmen and one tanker had no less than six destroyers, four corvettes, two antiaircraft ships, three minesweepers, three trawlers and two submarines to protect them. But this was not all. Further support was available, if needed, in the shape of two battleships, one carrier, six cruisers and 17 destroyers of the Home Fleet. The convoy set sail from Iceland on 27 June. Four days later Norway-based aircraft sighted it and U-boats began to shadow it. On 3 July the Admiralty learnt that the *Tirpitz*, with the heavy cruisers *Hipper* and *Scheer* in attendance, had slipped anchor. By now the convoy was under virtually constant air and U-boat attack. Next day, believing that the support group was too far away to counter the German squadron, the Admiralty ordered the convoy to scatter. The result was a massacre and only 10 ships eventually reached Archangel. The irony was that the *Tirpitz* never did make contact with the main convoy.

ABOVE LEFT: Hydroplane operators controlled the depth of U-boats.

ABOVE: *U-582* returns to Brest in August 1942 with a trophy, the ensign of the SS *Stella Dykes*, one of its victims. Two months later *U-582* herself would be sunk.

ABOVE LEFT AND LEFT: One of the most famous of the U-boat hunters, the sloop HMS *Starling*, and her skipper Frederick Walker (center) on his bridge during a U-boat hunt.

ABOVE: Arctic convoy PQ18 under air attack as seen from HMS *Avenger*.

RIGHT: One of PQ18's ammunition ships explodes after a direct hit, September 1942.

The immediate result was that the convoys were temporarily halted. When they resumed again at the beginning of September it was with even more escorts – PQ18 had no less than 16 destroyers and a carrier alone, apart from other types. The resources for this strengthening of protection could only come from the Atlantic. Toward the end of October there was to be another diversion, Operation Torch.

The forces taking part in the Allied landings in French North Africa were to come some from the United Kingdom and the remainder direct from the USA. These troop convoys required heavy escort and even the Russian convoys were virtually halted to ensure that this was provided. As it happened, the Axis were caught wrong-footed and the landings took place on 8 November 1942 with hardly a vessel lost during the long passages.

In December the Russian convoys began to be split into two in order to stretch the German resources.

Although the number of escorts was still very high, this new tactic, together with the facts that *Tirpitz* had left the theater at the end of October for a refit and German aircraft had been sent to reinforce the Mediterranean, meant that the convoys were managing to get through with much fewer casualties. A particularly encouraging sign came on the last day of the year when the cruiser and destroyer escort of JW51B saw off the *Hipper* and the *Lützow*, inflicting damage on the former in what was called the Battle of the Barents Sea. So angry was Hitler that he ordered the scrapping of the German surface fleet. Raeder resigned and was succeeded by Doenitz.

In the North Atlantic, on the other hand, the picture remained grim. There was only one bright spot. On 30 October *U-559* had been forced to the surface by destroyers and her crew surrendered. She herself sank, but not before a boarding party had been able to extract sufficient information from her Enigma machine for Bletchley Park to build a machine to reconstruct the daily Triton settings. By mid-December the U-boat Ultra signals were being read once more.

RIGHT: The hero of the Battle of the Barents Sea, Captain Robert Sherbrooke, VC, who successfully kept the *Admiral Hipper* and *Lützow* away from JW51B.

BELOW: Sherbrooke's destroyer, HMS *Onslow*, in the foreground.

ABOVE: The cruiser HMS *Sheffield* escorting a convoy en route to French North Africa for the Torch landings, November 1942.

RIGHT: The result of an attack on Russian convoy PQ18 – the destroyer *Harrier* transfers survivors of sunk merchantmen to the cruiser *Scylla*.

# THE TURNING POINT

In January 1943 President Roosevelt, Prime Minister Churchill and their military staffs met at Casablanca on the coast of Morocco in order to shape Allied strategy for the future. Apart from reaffirming the 'Germany first' policy and defining final victory as the unconditional surrender of the Axis powers, the conference made a number of other important decisions. Sicily was to be the next target for invasion, but planning was to go ahead for a major operation on the French coast and to this end Bolero, the build-up of US forces, was to continue with the aim of having over 900,000 troops in Britain by the end of the year. In order to ensure this it was recognized that the Battle of the Atlantic must be won, and quickly.

One of the first steps taken to reduce the U-boat menace was to turn the power of the strategic bombing forces based in Britain against them. Both the US Eighth Air Force and RAF Bomber Command were ordered to turn their attention on the Atlantic U-boat bases and on the U-boat building yards. It was not a success. Attacks on U-boat pens resulted in little damage to them, and certainly no U-boats were lost as a result. The cost of this was 76 bombers. The attacks against yards did little to slow production and cost a further 74 bombers. At the end of March 1943 Portal, the British Chief of the Air Staff, told the Anti-U-boat Committee that, while accepting that the results were disappointing, it merely showed that such diversions from attacks against German cities and industry were not worth it.

In the North Atlantic itself bad weather, together with the ability to read Triton, continued to keep the Allied losses down during January. Indeed, they fell to just over 200,000 tons. Even so, the Admiralty's monthly submarine report noted: 'A bolder and more ruthless strategy is now characteristic of the enemy. The tempo is quickening and the critical phase of the U-boat war in the Atlantic cannot be long postponed.' In February the bad weather continued, but the sinkings crept up to 315,000 tons.

Admiral Doenitz had taken over as the German naval commander-in-chief on 30 January. He persuaded Hitler to cancel his order to scrap the surface fleet, but retained tight control over the U-boats. A new operational policy was laid down. Instead of trying to catch both westbound and eastbound convoys, the U-boats were to concentrate on the latter. This made sense since they were more heavily laden than the westbound convoys, which had a significant proportion of ships in ballast. The wolf packs in the northwest Atlantic were to cover all possible convoy routes, while those in the northeast were to sweep westward, attacking those convoys previously engaged by the northwest packs and those which had managed to slip through the net. Westbound convoys would only be attacked on firm intelligence as to their whereabouts, or as specific targets of opportunity.

On 1 March the Western Allies convened the Atlantic Convoy Conference in Washington DC. The main pur-

PAGES 52-53: One of the main means of communication between ships at sea was the Aldis Lamp.

LEFT: The SS *Coulmore* negotiates the Atlantic in mid-winter.

ABOVE: U-boat pens at St Nazaire.

RIGHT: An escort carrier off Newfoundland. The aircraft on her flight deck are Grumman F6F Hellcats.

pose of this was to rationalize what had become a very complicated command structure. From now on, it was agreed, the responsibility for the North Atlantic would rest with just the British and Canadians, with the newly formed RCN North-West Atlantic Command taking responsibility for all convoy operations west of 47°W, which became the CHOP line, and Western Approaches covering east of this.

More very long-range aircraft would be based on Newfoundland and their operations were not to be restricted by the CHOP line. The US Navy would concentrate on the escort of tankers to and from the Dutch West Indies. It would, however, form a support group in the North Atlantic built round the escort carrier *Bogue*. The escort carrier was a concept that had been evolved in 1941 as a more efficient means to the CAM ship for giving convoys air cover. They were converted merchant ships and both the US and Royal Navies produced them. The concept of the support group was that it would be deployed to give extra help to any convoy under threat. This fitted in well with the views of the admiral commanding Western Approaches. Max Horton was one of the leading British submariners of 1914-18. He had assumed his present post in November 1942 and was convinced that the answer lay in more aggressive escort tactics. The sup-

port group was one of the measures that he had been advocating. These support groups, like the VLR aircraft, would not be restricted by the CHOP line.

The Atlantic Convoy Conference might have been expected to put new heart into the Allies, but it did not. The First Sea Lord and Chief of the Air Staff produced a joint memorandum for discussion by the Anti-U-boat Committee on 8 March. It began with the assumptions that every convoy must be regarded as under threat and that three convoys would be simultaneously under U-boat attack. It would be reasonable to forecast an exchange of one U-boat destroyed for every two merchantmen sunk, but then only if the escorts were made up of 12 ships — the current number was half this. Time was of the utmost importance. 'We are faced with the possibility of sustaining such heavy losses in individual convoys that we shall be forced to reduce the number of convoys in order to provide adequate escort. The import situation is such that this could not possibly be accepted.' Next day came even worse news. An additional rotor had been inserted in the U-boat Enigma machines and Bletchley Park considered that they would be unable to read Triton for some time to come, perhaps even months.

These gloomy predictions were borne out during the first three weeks of March. There was a sharp rise in

LEFT: A destroyer escort's twin 4.7 inch guns.

RIGHT: An escort engaging enemy aircraft attacking a convoy.

RIGHT: A Hedgehog launcher. Each projectile was filled with 32lbs of Torpex and they were fired together over the bows, producing a concentrated pattern at some 300 yards range.

sinkings. This was centered around the battle of Convoy SC121 at the beginning of the month, which suffered 13 ships sunk at no cost to the U-boats, and that involving HX229 and SC122 in the middle of March. In a series of desperate actions no less than 40 U-boats concentrated against these two convoys and sank 21 ships at a cost of just one of their own. The fact that Bletchley Park had begun to read Triton again from 12 March made little difference. Indeed, during the first three weeks of March the sinkings rose to over 500,000 tons, more than confirming the Admiralty's gloomy forebodings. If the spring gales had not then arrived the total would have been much higher.

What was clear to the Admiralty was that no longer could they rely on evading the wolf packs. Instead, the convoys would have to fight their way through them. This could only be done with strong escorts, but these were, as Churchill commented to Roosevelt, 'everywhere spread too thin.' An immediate decision was therefore

taken to cancel the next two Russian convoys. This made an additional 27 escort vessels and an escort carrier available and enabled a five further support groups to be formed. The first escort group, based on *Bogue*, had already proved its worth, enabling SC123 and HX230 to get through with the loss of just one straggler.

This marked the beginning of a new aggression in escort tactics. This was especially true since WATU at Derby House and the Submarine Tracking Room had realized that the key to success lay in dealing with the U-boat initially sighting the convoy. If it could be forced to dive the wolf pack would be blinded. Huff Duff would alert the escort to the sighting U-boat and radar would detect it on the surface.

During the first part of April the weather in the North Atlantic continued to be bad. There was also only one U-boat tanker available, which significantly reduced the number of U-boats on patrol in the area. Nevertheless, an indication that the new escort tactics showed

LEFT: *U-203*, a Type VIIC, leaves Brest on 3 April 1943 on her last cruise. On 25 April she was sunk by Swordfish aircraft from the escort carrier *Biter* and the destroyer HMS *Pathfinder*.

BELOW LEFT: The escort carriers *Avenger* and *Biter* during an Atlantic spring gale.

ABOVE RIGHT: The USS *Spencer* making a depth-charge attack. Note the full and empty depth-charge dischargers.

RIGHT: A U-boat after it had been caught on the surface by convoy escorts.

promise came during the battles between HX231 and Group *Löwenherz* (Lionheart) of 14 U-boats. In spite of there being a lull in the weather few of the U-boats which made contact with the convoy were able to get into a firing position, such was the aggression of the escort. Furthermore, 4th Support Group, built round the carrier *Biter*, was deployed in good time, thanks to Ultra, and air cover from Iceland was also able to play its part. The net result was that although six ships, including three stragglers, from the convoy were lost, two U-boats were sunk and four badly damaged.

Doenitz was, nevertheless, determined to build on his successes of March and as April wore on the number of U-boats in the North Atlantic increased. On the 19th the Submarine Tracking Room estimated that there were 53 U-boats present; a week later the figure had grown to 63. The stage was set for a climax and this would directly involve just one convoy, ONS5.

By spring 1943, eastbound fast (HX − 9-14 knots) and slow (SC − 7.5-9 knots) convoys were departing from Halifax, Nova Scotia, every three and six days respectively. Convoy planning for them rested with the US Navy Trade and Routeing Group and the Canadian National

Defense Headquarters at Ottawa, the convoys themselves being made up of a number of feeder convoys from Canadian and US ports. The westbound convoys (ON – fast, ONS – slow) were the responsibility of the Admiralty's Trade Division, but there was close coordination with the Americans and Canadians. These convoys usually left Liverpool every four (ON) and eight (ONS) days, but this frequency was alterable. Thus, on 28 April, because of the build-up of escort support groups, it was decided to extend ON sailing intervals to five and six days alternately and that for ONS convoys to 11 days.

Convoy composition was decided by the Naval Control Service and each port had a Naval Control Service Officer (NCSO), who assembled the ships for each convoy and, in the case of westbound convoys, informed Commander-in-Chief Western Approaches (CinCWA) through the NCSO in Liverpool. The convoy's route was worked out some 10 days before it sailed by the Admiralty Trade Division in consultation with the Submarine Tracking Room.

The feeder convoys had to be conducted by local escorts, usually converted trawlers, to the main convoy rendezvous. In the case of ONS5 these feeder convoys came from Liverpool, Milford Haven, Clyde, Oban and Londonderry. The vast majority of vessels were bound for Halifax and in ballast. Likewise, most of the ships were British, but some were flying the Norwegian, Panamanian, Greek, Dutch, Polish, US and Yugoslav flags.

Crucial in the preparation phase was the Convoy Conference. The NCSO acted as chairman and present, where applicable, would be a number of individuals representing a wide range of activities. The Convoy Commodore was a retired senior naval officer and was responsible for the discipline of the convoy as a whole and he would be accompanied at the conference by the masters of all the merchant vessels, together with their chief engineers. By this stage all merchant vessels were armed. Typical armament was that of the SS *Selvistan* (5136 tons), which sailed on ONS5. She had one 4in gun,

one 12pdr, two twin Lewis light machine guns, an Oerlikon AA gun and four signal rocket projectors. These weapons were manned by a mixture of Royal Navy and Royal Maritime Artillery gunners or, in the case of US vessels, by the US Navy Armed Guard. Their activities were coordinated by the convoy's Defense Equipment Merchant Ships (DEMS) officer, who was also present. The escort skippers, an RAF Coastal Command representative and the convoy signals officer also attended. It was at this conference that the final details were thrashed out.

When the convoy formed up, it did so in a standard formation. The ships were organized into columns of not more than four ships. Columns were usually some five cables (1000 yards) apart and within a column three cables (600 yards) separated ships. The commodore's vessel was always at the head of the center column and the oilers, of which ONS5 had two, also sailed in the center. A relatively new addition was the presence of two rescue trawlers. Usually certain merchant vessels, normally because they had good accommodation, were designated as rescue ships to look after the crews of torpedoed ships and sailed at the rear of the convoy. At the end of March 1943, however, Horton had asked the Admiralty for 13 ocean-going trawlers to be fitted out as rescue ships for slow convoys. Two of these, *Northern Gem* and *Northern Spray*, sailed with ONS5. They were also equipped for anti-submarine work and hence could be used as part of the escort.

At the time of the sailing of ONS5 there were 11 regular Mid-Ocean Escort Groups in the North Atlantic, operating out of Londonderry in Northern Ireland and St John's, Newfoundland. Seven were British (B1-B7) and four were Canadian (C1-C4). Other escort groups were from time to time deployed to the North Atlantic and the 40th Escort Group was present in addition in this capacity. These escort groups were very hardworking and seldom spent more than two weeks in port. Only when a vessel was undergoing repairs or a refit was there the

ABOVE RIGHT: A 20mm Oerlikon cannon crew. This was highly effective against both aircraft and U-boats.

LEFT: Heroes of the ONS5 battles – (left to right) Lt Cdr Hart, RN, (*Vidette*), Cdr Gretton, RN, (*Duncan*), Lt Cdr Plomer, RCNVR, (*Sunflower*).

opportunity for a longer break. When ONS5 sailed five groups were in port preparing to go out again while the remainder were at sea. Of the six support groups, four were at sea, one was at Argentia preparing to support HX235, which was about to sail, and the sixth would be ready for action on 29 April.

ONS5 was to be escorted by B7, whose Senior Officer of the Escort (SOE) was one of the crack escort skippers, Cdr Peter Gretton RN in *Duncan*, a D Class flotilla leader. It had been in existence for a year, although only one ship, the Flower Class corvette *Loosestrife*, was a founder member. The other ships in it were an old V Class World War 1 destroyer, *Vidette*, a River Class frigate, *Tay*, and three other corvettes, *Pink*, *Sunflower* and *Snowflake*. Most of the skippers were Royal Naval Reserve (RNR), but *Vidette*'s captain was a regular, like Gretton, and *Sunflower*'s was Royal Canadian Naval Volunteer Reserve (RCNVR).

The SOE was, in the words of the *Atlantic Convoy Instructions*, primarily charged with 'the safe and timely arrival of the convoy at its destination.' At the same time, if enemy forces were contacted, 'the escort shares with all other fighting units the duty of destroying enemy ships, provided this duty can be undertaken without due prejudice to the safety of the convoy.' The SOE was warned, however, that the enemy might well try to draw him away from the convoy. His command relationship with the convoy commodore could be tricky, especially as the latter invariably wore more rings on his sleeve. *Atlantic Convoy Instructions* stated that the SOE was 'responsible for the safety of the convoy from enemy action, but subject to his orders the commodore is to take charge of the convoyed ships.' While the commodore was responsible for the navigation of the convoyed

ships, the SOE was not to hesitate to warn the commodore if he considered that the convoy was 'standing to danger from a navigational point of view.' The SOE was also responsible for route alterations other than those ordered from above, but was to consult with the commodore 'if practicable.' The SOE was also enjoined to 'bear in mind the experience and knowledge of the commodore as to the capabilities of the ships of the convoy, and should refrain from interfering with the latter's desired disposition of ships in the convoy unless the convoy is in actual danger.' The other question was what happened if another officer senior to the SOE joined, something of especial relevance to support groups. Here the *Instructions* stressed that authority should remain with the SOE unless the support group commander had 'strong reasons' for not delegating the authority.

The air side was crucial. In the northeast Atlantic No 15 Group, RAF Coastal Command, was in charge. It had two Sunderland flying boat and one Liberator squadrons in Northern Ireland, two Sunderland squadrons at Oban, West Scotland, two B-17 Flying Fortress squadrons on Benbecula in the Hebrides, and one Hudson and one Liberator squadron in Iceland. On the other side of the Atlantic responsibility lay with the RCAF's Eastern Air Command which, like No 15 Group with CinCWA, was located with and under the operational control of North-West Atlantic Command at Halifax. This consisted of Nos 1 and 3 Groups, but only No 1 was directly involved in the Atlantic. This had one operational Canso squadron on Newfoundland and its two other squadrons, also on the island, were converting and non-operational. Also under command of No 1 Group were three USN squadrons at Argentia, with a small mixed detachment on Greenland and a Catalina squadron on Iceland,

LEFT: A Short Sunderland Mark III flying boat of 422 Squadron RCAF which was based at Oban in the Western Highlands of Scotland. The Sunderland had a maximum range of 2900 miles.

BELOW LEFT: A Consolidated Catalina flying boat, known as the Canso by the Canadians.

RIGHT: Maintenance work being carried out inside a Type IXB U-boat.

together with one Liberator and one B-17 squadron and a small mixed B-17/B-18 squadron of the US Army Air Forces Anti-Submarine Command and also stationed on Newfoundland.

Although the 'Black Gap' still existed, the aircraft involved were in the process of receiving new weapons and aids which would make them even more effective. In particular, there was Fido, an aerially delivered acoustic homing torpedo, and the ASV Mk3. This had a marked increase in range over the Mk2 (40 miles as against 12) and had a visual display. Perhaps more significant was that it could not be detected by Metox. Unfortunately, at least in the RAF and RCAF, it was a direct equivalent to RAF Bomber Command's H2S radar and had been delayed into Coastal Command service because Bomber Command had had priority of production. The Allied forces in the Battle of the Atlantic were therefore now in better shape than ever before, but then, in strength at least, so were the U-boats.

When Doenitz took over as CinC of the German Navy at the end of January 1943 he retained control over U-boat operations, moving the operational HQ from Paris to a hotel on the Steinplatz in Berlin. During the first quarter of 1943 U-boat production had peaked at 70 boats and by the end of April 140 of them were at sea. Of these half were in the North Atlantic. The bulk of the U-boats were still Type VIIs, but there were an increasing number of the longer range Type IXs. They were now armed with a new type of torpedo, the FAT, which had entered service at the end of 1942. This initially adopted a straight course, but then began to loop from left to right through 180°, which gave more chance of a hit when fired at a group of ships.

The torpedo dictated the U-boat tactics and at this stage in the war U-boats were encouraged to fire their torpedoes at ranges under 2000 meters to increase the chances of a hit. This meant getting inside the close escort screen, and a popular tactic was to attack from within the convoy itself. Normally all four bow tubes would be fired at once, and then, if need be, the stern tubes. The U-boat would then dive, wait until the convoy was a safe distance away, and then surface again to reload and catch up again. An alert and aggressive escort group would force the U-boat to engage from outside the screen, thus radically reducing the chances of a hit.

Doenitz did, however, have cause for concern. For a start, the mounting toll of U-boats sunk, now averaging 12 boats per month, meant that he had lost many of his veteran crews. Half the crews in the North Atlantic at the end of April 1943 were on their first operational cruise.

Hitler (decrypted by Bletchley Park) informing him that he had been awarded the Oakleaves to the Knight's Cross. By this time the Admiralty was becoming concerned over the threats building up in the path of ONS5 and ordered it to be rerouted farther north. In the meantime, a gale had sprung up, which made station keeping difficult, and two of Gretton's charges collided. On the 26th *Vidette* and her three charges joined the convoy and Doenitz ordered his packs to positions from where they could contact the next eastbound convoys. This, however, put them directly in the path of ONS5. Next evening Bletchley Park was suddenly unable to read Triton, probably because new settings had been introduced. The blackout would last until 5 May.

On 28 April the U-boats attempted to contact HX235 without success. Gretton located a U-boat on his Huff Duff, probably *U-377* reporting on HX235, but as a precaution CinCWA ordered him to adjust his course still farther to the north. Later that day ONS5 made a further Huff Duff contact. This was *U-650*, which began to shadow the convoy and called up the remainder of the newly formed *Star* group (15 boats). A US Navy Catalina from Squadron VP-84 on Iceland forced *U-650* to submerge and then sighted three other *Star* boats, attacking and damaging the bows of one. As dusk came, however, the contacts became more frequent and it became clear that attacks on the convoy were inevitable. The night was a busy one, but aggression and quick reactions by the escort prevented any ships being hit, although *Snowflake* had a narrow escape from a torpedo and one U-boat was slightly damaged.

By the morning of the 29th Horton realized that ONS5 was going to need reinforcement. Consequently, he signaled Flag Officer Newfoundland and asked him to despatch the 3rd Support Group (four Royal Navy destroyers) to meet the convoy. Another destroyer, *Oribi*, was also detached from 4th Support Group, which was assisting SC127. In the first few hours of daylight the U-boats had their first success, when *U-258* torpedoed the US vessel *Mckeesport*. She quickly fell behind and *Northern Gem* took off her crew before *U-258* later finished her off with two more torpedoes. Sadly, one of her seamen died that night - one problem was that rescue trawlers did not carry doctors — and he was buried at sea.

During 30 April the U-boats continued to shadow the convoy although the escorts succeeded in making them keep their distance. The weather began to worsen again and the immediate upshot of this was that air cover could no longer be provided from Iceland because of poor visibility. That night, with an increasing gale beginning to blow, there were further U-boat contacts and the escort fired a number of depth charges. By noon next day the gale had caused the convoy formation to break up and no less than 10 vessels had fallen behind and were straggling. The escorts did their best to round them up, but only managed to get two to rejoin the convoy by dusk, and this with the help of an RAF Iceland-based Liberator. B-24 Liberators from Greenland and Newfoundland were also in evidence. The weather did, however, prevent the U-boats from tackling the stragglers. *Specht* and *Amsel* were now ordered to concentrate on SC128, whose sailing from Halifax on the 28th had been picked up by the *B Dienst*.

The gale continued unabated during the 2nd. By this

More serious was the continuing realization that the Allies had a suspiciously accurate intelligence picture of the U-boat operations. Much of his evidence for this came from the successful reading of the daily Admiralty U-boat situation report which was transmitted to all SOEs. Yet he continued to refuse to believe that Triton might have been broken. Instead he became convinced that airborne radar was the cause, but there was little that he could do about this other than ordering the U-boats to submerge for 30 minutes if they became aware of radar transmissions.

On 22 April there were three major U-boat groups operating in the North Atlantic: *Specht* (Woodpecker — 17 boats) was operating against SC127, and *Meise* (Titmouse — 18 boats) against another eastbound convoy, HX 234. Group *Amsel* (Blackbird — 11 boats) was deploying to contact ONS4. At this time ONS5 had just formed up, but *Vidette* had been detached to Iceland to collect three additional ships to join the convoy.

*Specht* and *Meise* were generally frustrated by Greenland and Iceland-based aircraft, together with the carrier *Biter*'s aircraft, and two U-boats were sunk. On the 25th *U-404* (Cdr von Bülow) fired at *Biter* and claimed to have hit her, but his torpedoes exploded prematurely. That evening von Bülow received a personal signal from

time ONS5 was on the edge of the Greenland ice belt, and so an eye also had to be kept open for icebergs and pack ice. Further efforts were made to gather in the stragglers, again with some help from Iceland-based RAF Liberators. The bad weather meant that oiling was impossible and Gretton became increasingly concerned by *Duncan*'s rapidly decreasing fuel stocks. That evening 3rd Escort Group and *Oribi* joined and were sent to sweep ahead of the convoy. *Specht* and *Amsel* continued to await SC128, but this had been rerouted. Next day the gale raged with renewed intensity and in the afternoon Gretton decided that he could delay no longer. Handing over command of the escort to *Tay* (Lt Cdr Sherwood RNR), he made passage to St John's, arriving there two days later with just four percent fuel left in his tanks. At the same time, on orders of CinCWA, the destroyer *Impulsive* of 3rd Support Group left ONS5 to refuel at Iceland prior to joining SC128. Doenitz, still awaiting SC128, decided to adopt a new tactic. He split *Amsel* into four sub-groups, ordering the outer boats of each to transmit in order to give the impression of a continuous line right round the Newfoundland Banks. On one of the boats, *U-107*, there was cause for mild celebration amid the frustration and discomfort, when Engineer Schenk received a signal from his flotilla commander congratulating him on the birth of a son.

On 4 May the weather began to ease and Captain McCoy, commanding 3rd Escort Group, decided to send two of his destroyers to St John's to refuel since the seas were still too high to permit the oilers to be used. *Northern Gem* also left for the same destination to land her survivors. This left ONS5 with seven escorts with the main body and *Pink* some way astern shepherding four stragglers. The convoy had by now turned south and it became clear that a large concentration of U-boats was in its path, and no further route diversions were possible. Indeed Doenitz had now merged *Specht* and *Star* into a new group, *Fink* (Finch – 27 boats), and there was no way in which ONS5 could avoid it. Worse, south of this group lay the *Amsel* sub-groups. With the escort now so weakened, Horton ordered 1st Support Group (five sloops) to sail from St John's as reinforcement, but it would take two days' steaming to join ONS5. In the meantime the only bright spot was that the convoy was now in range of Canadian air cover. Two Canso sorties from Gander were launched that day to cover the convoy, but neither found it. Both attacked U-boats, however. The first contacted *U-630* from *Fink*, 30 miles west of ONS5. It dropped four depth charges and the U-boat disappeared, leaving a telltale oil slick and debris on the surface. As the pilot wrote in his combat report: '. . . all I can say is that after two-and-a-half years peering for "Subs" it really makes the pulse quicken when you finally click.' The other attack was against *U-438*, which decided to fight it out on the surface. The depth charges missed, but the aircraft's machine guns accounted for three of the crew before it was ordered back to base. As the afternoon wore on ONS5's escorts made an increasing number of Huff Duff contacts and that evening *U-628* made the first sighting of the convoy, which was thought to be ON180, expected in the area by dead reckoning, and not ONS5. Doenitz ordered *Fink* to attack – 'You are better placed than you ever were before.'

Shortly after midnight *U-707* opened the attack on ONS5 firing three torpedoes at the *North Britain*, which

sank in just two minutes. Only 11 crew members were saved by *Northern Spray*. *Vidette* then contacted *U-270*, inflicting some damage on her and forcing her to dive, but two other boats, *U-628* and *U-264*, managed to slip through the screen and quickly struck three more merchant vessels. *Northern Spray* managed to rescue 132 crew. Among them was Third Officer Skinner of the *Harbury* who was sunk for the fourth time. His first had been as a result of a mine, and then his ship had been hit by Japanese aircraft in the Indian Ocean. Rescued by another ship, this in turn was sunk by a Japanese cruiser. Just before dawn there were more explosions within the convoy and another two vessels were sent to the bottom. Thus, during the night six merchant vessels had been sunk and two U-boats damaged. The U-boats were now ordered to get ahead of the convoy once more and use the daylight hours for submerged attacks prior to another massive attack that night. 'The battle can't last long as the sea space left is short. So use every chance to the full, with all your might.'

During the morning there were numerous contacts, but since the sea was calm Sherwood decided to begin refueling some of the escorts. He successfully managed to take oil on board *Tay*, but *Oribi* was unable to refuel from the other oiler since her canvas hose broke. Just as *Oribi* took up station again there was another explosion and the merchantman *Dolius* settled and went to the bottom. During the afternoon *Offa* and *Oribi* were able to refuel from *British Lady*, which, her tanks now empty, then left for St John's. Efforts by Cansos to find the convoy were in vain, but Doenitz ordered that aircraft must not be allowed to thwart the attack. If contacted, U-boats were to stay on the surface and fight it out, with their attackers.

That evening the attacks began again. *U-266* opened the account, torpedoing three vessels, two of which remained afloat. *Offa*, however, managed to use her depth charges to good effect, forcing the U-boat to pull off for emergency repairs. An Iceland Liberator arrived and spent two-and-a-half hours with the convoy while survivors from the three ships were rescued. But, with over a quarter of the convoy now casualties and a large number of U-boats in the area, it seemed, as Captain McCoy later wrote, that convoy ONS5 'was threatened with annihilation.'

If the main body of the convoy was suffering, *Pink* and her stragglers had a rather better day. In the morning the escort obtained 'the sharpest and cleanest' ASDIC contact that her skipper had ever heard. Depth charges destroyed *U-192*. At the same time another straggler rejoined. Just as *Pink* was rejoining her charges she saw a column of smoke. It was the *West Makadet*, which had been torpedoed by *U-584*. *Pink* managed to keep the U-boat down and then rescued the crew before destroying the crippled merchantman with depth charges. That evening she had another contact, but dared not pursue it as otherwise the four stragglers would be left as easy meat for other U-boats.

Toward midnight the U-boats resumed their attacks on the main body in worsening visibility caused by fog. All the escorts made numerous contacts and, significantly, found themselves engaging some of these on the surface. First success was to *Loosestrife*, who engaged *U-638* on the surface with Oerlikon and 4in gunfire, forcing her to dive. She immediately fired a 10-pattern

ABOVE: Loading torpedoes into a U-boat was a complicated operation.

RIGHT: Caught napping. A U-boat, surprised on the surface by a Sunderland flying boat, suffers aerial depth-charge and machine-gun attack.

LEFT: *U-119*, a Type XB minelaying boat. She could carry 66 mines, but could also operate as a conventional U-boat, having two stern torpedo tubes. *U-119* was rammed and sunk by HMS *Starling* in late June 1943.

depth charge. The result was that 'submarine was observed to break surface, followed immediately by a violent explosion causing a vivid greenish-blue flash.' The U-boat's last signal was: 'Destroyer attacked. Sinking.'

Further surface contacts followed, but the subsequent engagements were inconclusive, until *Oribi* rammed *U-125* just aft of the conning-tower. Badly damaged, the U-boat limped away in the fog, calling for help. Six U-boats answered the call, but she was never found since two hours after the ramming she was spotted by *Snowflake*, which finished her off with gunfire. Some survivors were spotted in a dinghy, but Sherwood refused to allow *Snowflake*, covered by *Sunflower*, to pick them up since he could not afford any escort to be diverted at this very critical time. This was especially important since the contacts were still coming fast and furious. Indeed, while *Snowflake* was finishing off *U-125*, *Vidette* engaged another U-boat with a Hedgehog salvo. This marked the end of *U-531*. Immediately afterward *Sunflower* rammed *U-533* as she crash dived, dropping two depth charges as she passed over her. In spite of the damage, the U-boat did eventually manage to limp back to base. A little later, *Loosestrife* contacted another U-boat in the rear of the convoy and saw it off with gunfire and depth charges. This was the last contact by B7 or 3rd Support Group, but not the end of the battle.

1st Support Group was steaming in line abreast and by dawn on 6 May was rapidly closing on ONS5. They located the convoy on radar at a range of eight miles, but just after doing so, *Pelican* contacted a U-boat on her radar. A few minutes later her wake was sighted at 400 yards. *Pelican* opened fire and the U-boat began to crash dive. Depth charges were fired and *U-438*'s life was ended. The final contact was made by *Spey* on *U-634*,

which eventually managed to escape, although badly damaged.

That afternoon Western Local Escort Group W4 (three RCN corvettes and a minesweeper) met the main body and took over the escort and B7 sailed to St John's. Before he did so Sherwood signaled CinCWA that there had been 24 attacks on the convoy during the night, but none had been successful and five U-boats were claimed as sunk. A great victory had been snatched from the jaws of defeat and there was understandable jubilation in Liverpool, London, Ottawa and St John's. Even Churchill was moved to signal Sherwood: 'My compliments to you on your unceasing fight against the U-boats. Please pass to commodore of convoy my admiration for the steadfastness of his ships.'

In contrast, on the Steinplatz in Berlin there was increasing gloom as reports of sunk and damaged U-boats flowed in. On the morning of 6 May Doenitz acknowledged defeat in this particular convoy battle and ordered *Fink* and *Amsel* Groups to withdraw. Of the 41 U-boats which had engaged ONS5 during 4-6 May no less than six were sunk and 10 damaged. The Germans concluded that their failure against the convoy had been because of the weather, radar, air cover and the increased number of escorts, and that 'at the moment U-boat operations are more difficult than ever before.' The next two weeks served to confirm this.

HX237, in spite of the efforts by two wolf packs to get to grips with it, got through with the loss of three stragglers but accounted for three more U-boats. It was the same with SC129, where the exchange was two U-boats for two merchant vessels. ONS7 lost just one ship to a U-boat, which in turn was promptly sunk. Worse, SC130, escorted by B7, with Gretton in a hurry to get

ABOVE: Distinguished by its white fuselage, a maritime patrol Consolidated Vultee Liberator over England. It was the employment of this aircraft in sufficient numbers which eventually closed the Black Gap.

RIGHT: Maritime air power claims another victim. Note the depth charge falling in lower right-hand corner.

home for his wedding, lost no ships and the escorts, supported once more by 1st Support Group and the Liberators of 120 Squadron RAF, sank four U-boats and badly damaged two others. ON178 and HX239 also got through unscathed, with the loss of a further two U-boats and one badly damaged.

By 22 May 32 U-boats had been lost since the beginning of the month, two-thirds of them in the North Atlantic. Doenitz called it 'a frightful total, which came as a hard and unexpected blow.' Accordingly, he ordered U-boat operations to cease in the North Atlantic, withdrawing his boats to southwest of the Azores. On the last day of the month, by which time a further nine boats had been lost, he went to see Hitler at his mountain retreat at Berchtesgaden to explain. He reassured the Führer that new technical aids were on their way and with these the battle, on which depended 'the outcome of the war,' would be won.

The effect of the withdrawal of the U-boats was dramatic. In June shipping losses in the North Atlantic fell to their lowest since the beginning of the war, a mere 30,000 tons from all causes. That same month, for the first time in the war, the rate of new launchings of merchant ships exceeded losses. The tide was clearly on the turn, but it was those 36 hours during 4-6 May when ONS5 fought back from the brink of disaster to send the U-boats away, bruised and dispirited, that the decisive turning point in the Battle of the Atlantic came.

# THE ENDLESS BATTLE

If Doenitz was having major problems in the North Atlantic during mid-summer 1943, there was a renewed threat to that maritime U-boat bottleneck, the Bay of Biscay. Air Chief Marshal Sir John Slessor, commanding RAF Coastal Command, recognized the importance of the Bay in a memorandum which he addressed to the British Chiefs of Staff in April 1943: 'The Bay of Biscay is the trunk of the Atlantic U-boat menace, the roots being in the Biscay ports and the branches spreading out far and wide.' He was therefore given permission to mount another Bay offensive in May. In contrast to the 1942 offensive, the aircraft were very much better equipped, especially in the ASV Mk3, which could not be detected by Metox. Five U-boats were sunk in the Bay during May, and this rose to 11 in July.

Doenitz responded by further increasing the anti-aircraft armament on his U-boats and even tried sending them through the Bay in convoys. Ultra's ability to indicate when the U-boats were leaving port helped the British considerably and, convinced that Metox must be giving away the U-boat's position, Doenitz banned its use at the beginning of August. One reason for him doing this was that a captured RAF pilot had told his interrogators that RAF Coastal Command seldom used their radars actively since Metox transmissions could be detected up to 90 miles. A total untruth, but Doenitz, grasping at straws, chose to believe it. That month, however, such was the air threat that he was forced to resort to his original tactic of sending his boats through the Bay singly by night. This meant that far fewer could be deployed to the Atlantic. Indeed, only 20 made the passage in August, closely hugging the Spanish coast before turning west into the Atlantic itself, compared to four times this number who had previously crossed the Bay each month. One other significant measure that the Allies took was to introduce a new secure BAMS cipher so that no longer would the U-boats be able to gain convoy intelligence from this source.

As early as 1934 development work had begun on an acoustic homing torpedo. The original idea was to produce a torpedo with a speed greater than 30 knots for use against warships. At the beginning of the war other priorities slowed down research and development into it, and the requirement was modified to a 20 knot torpedo for use against merchant vessels. In late autumn 1942 this materialized as the G7es *Falke* (Falcon), which had a range of 5-7km and could engage ships traveling at 7-13 knots from a bearing of 0-180°. The homing equipment meant that the warhead was much smaller than the conventional torpedo, and *Falke* could not be used in the tropics. During February-March 1943 six U-boats were equipped with it for operational trials. Its first success came on 23 February, when *U-382* sank a tanker, part of Convoy UC1. During the trial only three *Falke* were actually fired, but two out of the three obtained hits. After some modification *Falke* was declared ready for operational service on 1 July 1943.

The heavy U-boat losses of May 1943 made Doenitz and his staff realize that it was imperative to develop, and quickly, a torpedo which would be effective against escort vessels. This needed to run at a much higher speed and had to have a proximity fuze to cater for the shallower draught of a warship. The fuze presented technical difficulties and the scientists did not believe that they could produce a reliable weapon until the beginning of 1944. Doenitz was adamant. On 13 July he demanded that this torpedo, called the *Zaunkönig* (Wren), be ready for operations by 1 August. Believe it or not, 80 were ready by that date. With a speed of 24.5 knots, it was capable of successfully engaging a ship steaming at 10-18 knots at a range of some 5km.

At the beginning of September 1943, the U-boats, equipped with their new acoustic torpedoes, were ordered back to the North Atlantic. Their first targets, identified by *B Dienst*, were the westbound convoys ONS18 and ON202. During the period 19-23 September,

in a series of air-sea and surface-sub-surface clashes, a destroyer and two corvettes, together with six merchantmen, were sunk, and a further escort badly damaged. Three U-boats were destroyed. The inevitably exaggerated reports that reached Doenitz that three destroyers and 12 merchantmen had been sunk, raised both his and Hitler's hopes. These were quickly dashed when the U-boats moved to intercept further convoys. They sank one destroyer, but lost three of their own to Iceland-based Liberators. In a further five-day battle with two convoys there were even worse results, with just one merchant vessel being sunk and six U-boats destroyed. Worse, it was becoming increasingly noticeable that the U-boat crews were lacking in confidence because of the high casualty rate. This was manifested by a marked tendency not to press home attacks. By mid-November Doenitz felt forced once more to withdraw his boats from the North Atlantic.

In contrast, the Allies moved from strength to strength. The build-up of VLR maritime patrol aircraft enabled the 'Black Gap' to be finally eradicated. Anti-submarine tactics became even more aggressive. With more escort carriers now available they were able to revert to the original British concept of hunter-killer groups built round carriers. Four of these were operational by autumn 1943. An antidote to the acoustic torpedo was quickly introduced. This was a drogue, which produced noises similar to a ship's engine and was towed by the escort. Against the deep-diving U-boat a new escort drill was developed. One ship located the position of the submerged U-boat through ASDIC and passed this to the other escorts who were steaming silently in the area. They then fired patterns of depth charges, set to explode deep, in the U-boat's track. So effective was the ploy that no U-boat subjected to this form of attack survived to tell the tale.

The dramatic increase in Allied fortunes in the Atlantic during the summer and early autumn of 1943 meant that the challenge of the Russian convoys could be faced once more. The original intention had been to resume them in spring 1943, but the need to secure the sea routes in the North Atlantic took precedence. In addition to this *Tirpitz*, accompanied by *Scharnhorst* and *Lützow*, returned to northern Norway in March. The Sicily landings further delayed recommencement of the convoys, and matters were not helped by the Russians demanding the closure of two British radio stations at Murmansk.

As a necessary preliminary to reopening the northern route the *Tirpitz* and her two consorts had to be neutralized and a plan was made to attack her in her anchorage in the Altenfjord near North Cape using midget submarines known as X-craft. On 8 September, shortly before this could be put into operation, *Tirpitz* and *Scharnhorst* made a brief foray to bombard the weather station on Spitzbergen. *Scharnhorst*'s captain considered that his crew needed more gunnery practice and so put to sea again almost immediately. At the same time, *Lützow* moved to a new anchorage. Consequently, when, on 22 September, the X-craft entered Altenfjord only *Tirpitz* was present. Six X-craft had been trained for the task, but two broke their tow on passage and were lost. Two of the remainder succeeded in fixing charges to the *Tirpitz*, wrecking her engines, buckling her rudder and putting two turrets out of action. The X-craft crews were all killed or captured. The day after the attack *Lützow* returned to Germany for a refit. This left just the *Scharnhorst* and five destroyers to challenge the Russian convoys, which finally began to sail again in mid-November.

The CinC of the Home Fleet, Admiral Sir Bruce Fraser, hoped to be able to use the convoys to tempt the *Scharnhorst* out so that he could destroy her. It was a month before his plan worked. On 22 December German aircraft spotted Convoy JW55B and the *Scharnhorst* put to sea. In order to trap her Fraser had sailed in the battle-

PAGES 68-69: An RAF Coastal Command Mosquito engaging a U-boat.

LEFT: An X-craft, one of the type which made the daring attack on the *Tirpitz* in the Altenfjord.

RIGHT: The battleship HMS *Duke of York* which flew Admiral Sir Charles Fraser's flag in the Battle of the North Cape.

ship *Duke of York*, supported by a cruiser and four destroyers, and also a further force of three cruisers. On 26 December the latter contacted *Scharnhorst* and exchanged shots with her. In the meantime, Fraser had maneuvered to cut off the German ship's withdrawal to Altenfjord. Late that afternoon he spotted her and after a two-and-a-half hour battle sank her. Only 36 of her crew were rescued.

The Battle of North Cape finally removed the surface threat to the Russian convoys. The fear remained, though, that *Tirpitz* might be refurbished and throughout most of 1944 a number of attempts were made to destroy her by air attack. Eventually, on 12 November, she was attacked by 9 and 617 Squadrons of RAF Bomber Command and turned turtle. The air and sub-surface threats still remained, but between August 1944 and April 1945 no fewer than 250 Allied merchant vessels would make the passage to the northern Russian ports, carrying more than one million tons of war *matériel*.

When Doenitz withdrew his wolf packs from the North Atlantic in mid-November 1943 he redeployed them to attack the Gibraltar convoys, many of which were carrying *matériel* to support the Allied forces in Italy. His hopes of easier pickings were quickly disillusioned. On 17 November, a Luftwaffe aircraft spotted a convoy of 60 ships steaming north some 400 miles off the Spanish coast. Next day the U-boats made contact, but lost one of their number rammed in exchange for the disablement of an escort by *Zaunkönig* torpedo. Doenitz ordered further boats to be concentrated against the convoy, but his orders were picked up by Ultra and the escort streng-

LEFT: A damaged Fleet Air Arm Barracuda is held by arrester wires after returning from an attack on the *Tirpitz*.

BELOW LEFT: The director station on the cruiser *Saumarez* after taking a hit from the *Scharnhorst* during the Battle of the North Cape.

RIGHT: The corvette *Honeysuckle* in Murmansk after the arrival of convoy JW65, March 1945.

BELOW: The *Tirpitz* under repair, July 1944.

BELOW RIGHT: A Swordfish warms up on the escort carrier *Fencer*.

thened, as well as continuous air cover provided. During the next few days, try as they might, the U-boats could not penetrate the screen, which destroyed three of them. During the next few weeks, other wolf packs suffered similar failures. Eventually, on 7 January 1944, Doenitz was forced to the conclusion that wolf pack tactics were counter-productive. From now on U-boats would be deployed singly. There were, however, in the pipeline new breeds of U-boat which could yet restore Germany's shattered naval fortunes.

The U-boat was at its most vulnerable when on the surface, and increasingly so in view of Allied air dominance of the Atlantic. The two main reasons why a U-boat had to surface were because its slow underwater speed made it impossible to keep pace with a convoy and also because it needed to recharge its batteries.

The conventional submarine was powered by a diesel engine, but this would not operate underwater and when submerged the boat was propelled by electric power. As early as the beginning of 1933 the German scientist Professor Hellmuth Walter had begun to seriously consider the design of a high-speed submarine capable of underwater speeds of up to 30 knots. His idea was to use hydrogen peroxide in order to break down water into a high pressure, oxygen-based gas which would drive a turbine to propel the submarine through the water. In early 1940 he produced a small experimental prototype, which achieved underwater speeds of just over 24 knots, but not until two years later was Walter able to persuade the German Navy to take more than polite interest in his concept. The reason for this was that it was seen as a distraction to the production of the conventional Type VII and Type IX U-boats, the rate of which had to be increased if the Battle of the Atlantic was to be won.

Doenitz, however, recognized the potential of the Walter boat and by the end of 1942 work had begun on a coastal U-boat, with range sufficient to operate in the North Sea. This was to become the Type XVII. At the same time Doenitz demanded that an ocean-going version be designed, which was to be classified as the Type XVIII. The main problem with the Walter boat was that the hydrogen peroxide was expensive to produce and highly unstable. The problem of safely storing it on board took time to overcome, and there were also mechanical teething troubles and shoddy production processes. As a result, the Walter boats never did enter service before the end of the war. If they had done so in any numbers, their ability to achieve submerged speeds of up to 24 knots would have given the Allies severe problems in dealing with them.

ABOVE: Type XXIII electro-coastal boats. *U-2336* set out on her first patrol on 1 May 1945, returning to port two weeks later after having sunk two ships.

ABOVE RIGHT: Another success for 10 Squadron, Royal Australian Air Force.

LEFT: Type XXI ocean-going boats. Only one of the 123 completed before the end of the war was deployed operationally.

Another method of remaining submerged for longer was the Schnorkel, a tube which could introduce atmospheric air to the diesel engine while the boat was just below the surface. Walter had considered the idea in 1933 as part of his high-speed concept, but it was the Royal Netherlands Navy who first put the idea into practice and two of their submarines were equipped with it by the outbreak of war. Not until March 1943 did Walter consider the idea again and raise it with Doenitz, arguing that it would make the U-boats harder to detect by radar. The tube itself would have to be collapsible. Prototypes were first fitted to training boats and then to two Type VIIs. The early trials were successful, but operational crews took some convincing, fearing that if they got the safe cruising depth just slightly wrong they might all be poisoned. During winter 1943-44 the introduction of the Schnorkel onto existing operational boats proceeded slowly, and crew confidence was not increased by the loss of the first to be so fitted, *U-264*, in the North Atlantic on 19 February 1944 on her first cruise. Nevertheless, confidence did grow during summer 1944 as Schnorkel fitted boats began to have some success. The main problem was that a speed of 5-6 knots only could be achieved with it, which meant much more time on passage and less on patrol. On the other hand, it certainly reduced casualties since no longer did the boats have to surface to recharge batteries.

High-speed submerged travel could be achieved in another way than the Walter method. This was by radically increasing the number of batteries carried, coupled to high-powered motors. Streamlining the hull and cutting out most of the bridge superstructure, guns and other protruberances also helped. The result of this was the Type XXI (coastal) and Type XXIII (ocean-going) electro-boats. These were capable of submerged speeds of up to 17 knots for 30 minutes before having to rise to Schnorkel depth to recharge. The first of each type entered service in June 1944, but not before the Allies had invaded France.

The Allies were well aware of the serious threat that the U-boats could pose to the Overlord forces as they crossed the English Channel to Normandy. Accordingly they had gathered together a number of escort carriers and no fewer than 286 smaller anti-submarine craft to protect the invasion fleet. Overhead 21 anti-submarine squadrons unceasingly patrolled the skies above the Bay of Biscay. In the early hours of 6 June Doenitz ordered his Biscay U-boats to leave port to attack the Allied invasion shipping, a signal that was promptly intercepted by Ultra. The massive Allied air presence soon forced those not equipped with Schnorkel back to port. As for the remainder, they inched their way slowly north. Not until

ABOVE: Landing supplies on the Normandy beaches. The failure of the U-boats to make any impression on the invasion forces was a major reverse.

ABOVE RIGHT: A U-boat construction yard at Bremen pictured just after the end of the war.

LEFT: An escort destroyer and escort carrier in the North Atlantic.

nine days later did the first, *U-621*, arrive off the Cherbourg peninsula. After sinking a US transport and missing two US battleships it began the wearisome voyage back to port. Three more arrived by the end of June, but again successes were few. Indeed, out of 30 boats deployed, 20 were sunk.

Once the Allies were secure in the Normandy beachhead the end of the war could only be a matter of time, especially given the devastating Soviet summer offensive on the Eastern Front. Increasing U-boat sinkings – during July-September 1944 these rose to 79 – and a decline in the commissioning of new boats, brought about largely by the increasing intensity of the Anglo-US strategic bombing campaign, meant that the writing was on the wall. The new electro-boats had some successes, but there were simply not enough to cause significant damage. By the last quarter of 1944 the average daily number of U-boats on operational patrol had declined from 110 to 35 over the first quarter of 1943.

Yet there were still dedicated U-boat crews who would fight on until the bitter end. On 7 May 1945, the day before victory in Europe (VE), came their last two successes when Schnorkel equipped Type VIIs, *U-2303* and *U-2306*, respectively sank the British freighters *Snea*

*land I* and *Avondale Park* off the Firth of Forth. By that stage the construction yards in the Baltic and North Sea had been overrun and the Biscay ports, which Hitler had declared as *Festungs* (fortresses) in July 1944, were surrendering. Two days before this Doenitz, now Führer of the ruins of the Third Reich sent his last signal to his U-boats, some 40 of which were still at sea:
'My U-boat men!
Six years of U-boat war lie behind us. You have fought like lions. A crushing material superiority has forced us into a narrow area. A continuation of our fight from the remaining basis is no longer possible.
U-boat men! Undefeated and spotless you lay down your arms after a heroic battle without equal. We remember in deep respect our fallen comrades, who have sealed with death their loyalty to Führer and Fatherland.
Comrades! Preserve your U-boat spirit, with which you have fought courageously, stubbornly and imperturbably through the years for the good of the Fatherland.
Long Live Germany!'

Most greeted this order to lay down their arms with relief, but some could not bear the thought. A few boats made for neutral harbors, two sailed to Argentina and a further five to Japan. The remainder returned to port over the next two weeks and surrendered to the Allies.

No other campaign in World War II lasted quite as long as the Battle of the Atlantic, which began on 3 September 1939 with the sinking of the *Athenia* and ended on 7 May 1945 with the last two merchant vessels being sent to the bottom. The cost to both sides was enormous. The Germans had in existence at the beginning of the war, and commissioned during it, just under 1200 U-boats. Of these no less than 782 were sunk. To this must be added the losses in surface ships and aircraft. No less than 23 million tons of Allied shipping were destroyed, 15 million tons of which were in the North Atlantic. The pendulum of fortune had swung one way and then the other in what had been a prolonged and agonizing wrestling match of human and technical endeavor.

BELOW: Admiral Sir Max Horton, CinC Western Approaches, inspects *U-532*, which had been on her way back from Japan with a cargo of tin, quinine, wolfram and rubber prior to its capture.

RIGHT: Surrending U-boats being escorted into Londonderry, Northern Ireland.

## ACKNOWLEDGMENTS

The author and publishers would like to thank Ron Callow for designing this book and Ron Watson for compiling the index. The following agencies provided photographic material:

**Bison Books,** pages: 2, 6, 10(bottom), 11(both), 12, 14(top & middle), 15(top), 19(bottom), 24, 30(all three), 35(top two), 50(bottom), 62(both), 74(both).

**Bundesarchiv,** pages: 1, 10(top), 16(top), 22(bottom), 23(top), 29(bottom), 33(top), 43(top), 44, 48(both top), 55(top), 58(top), 63, 66.

**Hulton-Deutsch Collection,** pages: 17(top), 22(top), 56(top), 57(top), 61, 78(top).

**Robert Hunt Library,** pages: 7, 16(bottom), 18, 21(bottom), 26, 27(both), 28(both), 31(both), 32, 34(top), 35(middle), 37(both), 38(bottom), 39, 40-41, 42(bottom), 43 (bottom), 45, 46, 47(both), 49(bottom), 50(top), 51(bottom), 54, 55(bottom), 57(bottom), 58(bottom), 59(both), 65(top), 67(bottom), 70, 72(top), 73(bottom left), 75, 76(bottom), 77.

**Imperial War Museum, London,** pages: 4, 8(top), 9(both), 14(bottom), 17(bottom), 20, 21(top), 23(bottom), 28(bottom), 29(middle), 33(bottom), 35(bottom), 36(bottom), 48(bottom both), 49(top), 51(top), 52-3, 60, 65(bottom), 68-9, 71, 72(bottom), 73(top & bottom right), 78(bottom).

**National Maritime Museum, London,** page: 19(top).

**US Defense/Naval Photographs,** page: 8(bottom).

**US National Archives,** pages: 15(bottom), 38(top), 67(top), 76(top).

**WZ-Bildienst,** pages: 16(top), 29(top), 34(bottom).